SPIRIT WEAVER

Wisdom Teachings
from the
Feminine Path *of* Magic

Seren Bertrand

Bear & Company
Rochester, Vermont

Bear & Company
One Park Street
Rochester, Vermont 05767
www.BearandCompanyBooks.com

Bear & Company is a division of Inner Traditions International

Cataloging-in-Publication Data for this title is available from the Library of Congress

ISBN 978-1-59143-435-1 (print)
ISBN 978-1-59143-436-8 (ebook)

Printed and bound in the United States by Versa Press, Inc.

10 9 8 7 6 5 4 3 2 1

Text design and layout by Priscilla Harris Baker
This book was typeset in Garamond Premier Pro with Blacker, Celestial, Futura, Gill Sans, Trenda, and Walpurgis Night used as display typefaces

Well dressing photo on page 12 by Greg Balfour Evans / Alamy Stock Photo; well dressing photo on page 64 by DeFacto, CC BY-SA 4.0, via Wikimedia Commons; king photo on page 66 by Somewhere in the world today..., CC BY 2.0, via Flickr; king and consort photo on page 67 by Donald Judge, CC BY 2.0, via Flickr; maypole photo on page 68 and posies photo on page 69 by Somewhere in the world today..., CC BY 2.0, via Flickr.

To send correspondence to the author of this book, mail a first-class letter to the author c/o Inner Traditions • Bear & Company, One Park Street, Rochester, VT 05767, and we will forward the communication, or contact the author directly at **www.serenbertrand.com**.

SPIRIT WEAVER

"Feminine magic is a spiritual wisdom that lives inside of us. In *Spirit Weaver,* Seren Bertrand brings together the threads of body, memory, lineage, identity, and nature to restore our innate capacity as the ones who weave with spirit. The time is now to reclaim our feminine magic for co-creating our lives and healing our world—what a gift Seren has bestowed in this treasury of feminine knowledge."

TAMI LYNN KENT, AUTHOR OF *WILD FEMININE,*
WILD CREATIVE, AND *MOTHERING FROM YOUR CENTER*

"Now more than ever we need a deeper connection to the earth, spirit realm, and our sacred bodies. Seren brings us valuable wisdom at a time when more and more women are fighting disease from a disconnection to the Divine. Her womb wisdom and research are inspiring, eloquent, and soul filling."

SHIVA ROSE, AUTHOR OF *WHOLE BEAUTY*

"Drawing on ancient myths as well as the author's own life experiences, Bertrand guides you home to the authentic everyday magic of the divine feminine that is your birthright. This magic is deeply connected to the earth and as close as our kitchen-table gatherings. *Spirit Weaver* offers inspiration and wisdom. It is a book you'll be wise to keep close at hand."

ROBIN ROSE BENNETT, AUTHOR OF
THE GIFT OF HEALING HERBS AND *HEALING MAGIC*

FOR MUM AND ORPHEA

Spirit of Avalon

Contents

INTRODUCTION **Welcome Inside**   1
The Great Weave

Spinning Our Web

1   **Spirit Weaving**   17
Path of Feminine Magic

2   **Feminine Power**   25
Awaken Your Spiritual Womb

3   **Womb Revolution**   31
Women's Body Magic

4   **Cosmic Birth**   34
Dragon Priestesses of Earth

5   **Moon Mysteries**   39
Lunar Cycles of Wisdom

6   **Menstrual Magic**   41
Restoring Our Balance

7   **Moon Mystic**   45
The Mysteries of Midnight

8   **Feminine Alchemy**   47
Embracing Transformation

| 9 | **Spirit Keepers of the Womb** | 49 |
| | *Water Bearers, Fire Keepers* | |

| 10 | **Magic Studies** | 54 |
| | *Feminine Mystery Schools* | |

Growing Our Roots

| 11 | **Mother Mountain** | 58 |
| | *Land of the Grail Goddess* | |

| 12 | **Domestic Witchery** | 71 |
| | *Creating Your Nest* | |

| 13 | **Rooted Power** | 77 |
| | *Feminine Spiritual Path* | |

| 14 | **Endarkenment** | 82 |
| | *God Is in the Soil* | |

| 15 | **Grandmother Wisdom** | 84 |
| | *Our Primordial Knowing* | |

| 16 | **Crone Blessings** | 87 |
| | *Celebrating Our Elders* | |

| 17 | **Celtic Magic** | 89 |
| | *Path of the Swan Priestess* | |

| 18 | **Spirit Birds** | 93 |
| | *Song of the Feminine Christ* | |

| 19 | **Soul Fertility** | 99 |
| | *Our Audacious Creativity* | |

| 20 | **Primordial Devotion** | 104 |
| | *How the Feminine Prays* | |

WEAVING OUR HEALING

21 **Wild Feminine** 108
Dreaming with Mother Earth

22 **Underworld Journey** 111
The Descending Path

23 **Witch Wound** 114
Reclaiming Our Wisdom

24 **Shadow Healing** 117
Rebirthing the Feminine

25 **Lamentations** 122
The Shamanic Pathway of Grief

26 **Soft Power** 126
The Magic of Vulnerability

27 **Healing Hands** 129
Opening Your Heart

28 **Motherline Magic** 131
Healing Our Maternal Legacy

29 **Yoni Temple** 137
Healing Sacred Feminine Rituals

30 **Feminine Archetypes** 143
The Witch and the Priestess

DREAMING OUR MAGIC

31 **Womb of the World** 146
Circle of the Ancestors

32 **Dakini Magic** 153
Jewel in the Lotus Womb

33   **Goddess Initiation**   160
The Power of Kali

34   **Lady Saturn**   163
Lineage of the Cosmic Witch

35   **Scarlet Woman**   169
Temple of the Feminine Arts

36   **Priestess Path**   172
Story of the Holy Whore

37   **Prince of Scorpio**   175
The Dancing Magician

38   **Ecstatic Mystics**   178
The Passion of Teresa of Ávila

39   **Metatron Magic**   183
Dragons of Creation

40   **Quantum Leaps**   186
The Mysteries of Time

Enchanting Our World

41   **Eclipse Magic**   191
The Lion and the Mermaids

42   **Dream Wisdom**   196
Awakening the Psyche

43   **Soul Alchemy**   199
Merging Power and Love

44   **Biology of Bonding**   204
Sacred Union and Soulmates

45   **Opening to Love**   207
Descending into the Heart

46   **Romantic Love**   212
A Mystical Spiritual Path

47   **Christ Magic**   215
The Goddess of Avalon

48   **Epiphany**   221
Three Wise Witchy Midwives

49   **Nativity Mystery**   229
Gateway of the Mother

50   **Witches' Rebirth**   237
Baba Yaga's Initiation

Closing Prayer   241

About the Author and the Illustrator   242

Welcome Inside

The Great Weave

Awen a ganaf, Odwfn ys dygaf
(I sing awen, I bring it forth from the deep)

Bardic invocation

"Ours is only a little power, seems like, next to theirs," Moss said. "But it goes down deep. It's all roots. It's like an old blackberry thicket. And a wizard's power's like a fir tree, maybe, great and tall and grand, but it'll blow right down in a storm. Nothing kills a blackberry bramble."

Ursula K. Le Guin, *Tehanu*

Welcome dear readers,

I am happy to share this book with you, and I hope it lands in your life like a blessing. Imagine that this collection of essays is a weaving river. Dip in where you feel called, and soak up a little bit of simple feminine magic. We need this magic now more than ever. We've been "doing the work," but we also need to be the beauty. Feminine magic is a homecoming to our true nature.

These essays are not here to teach you or to tell you but to sprinkle a little fairy dust over you. Keep this book by your bedside or on your kitchen table to flick through when you need a little lift.

· · · · · a Bun dance · · · · · ·

This is your witch's treasury, which brings an everyday grace to your life, no big effort needed. We need this simplicity and sense of grace and blessing. Remember, you are always blessed.

Spirit keeping is about a deep connection with the land, the story of the land, and the stories kept within our body—and the weave between people and the land, which keeps on being rewoven.

Everything I've learned is from the memory and the stories told by the land, and the stories of my body that can have a cup of tea and a chat with the slow earth vibration that hums and exists right underneath our busy modern world. This other world is not just another time that's long gone in the past but another dimension existing right now when we slow down and reconnect. So these stories and love notes are humming with all the places I've visited and the stories I've journeyed through during the seven years

I wrote them, including the memories of those spirit keepers who've now passed into rainbow land and those who are still holding the thread.

These stories were mostly woven together between 2012 and 2018 when I was holding space for a global feminine mystery school and weaving with a circle of womb oracles, whose wisdom brought up new questions and ideas to take to the land, so Earth could share what she knew.

Looking back now, we can see that between 2012 and 2019 the world was in an in-between space, a time out of time, in betwixt the worlds, as prophecies had predicted. In the spirit weave of lore, an old world died on the winter's eve of 2012, and the new world didn't take shape or form until 2020, catapulting us into a massive dissolution as the new birth started in earnest.

Mayan astrology predicted that the initial gateway to a new cycle would open on winter solstice 2012, but that the real bolt through the gate would happen on winter solstice 2019. In those liminal seven years in between, the veils were very thin and the ancestors were speaking, and I, boarded on a wombship sailing from one old world to a new land, was listening carefully. These essays are infused with that listening, so the ancestors' words can keep speaking to us now.

 ## Awen, Avalon, Swan Ladies

This ancestral voice calling me into a deeper relationship with spirit weaving began as we were about to enter 2012. I wasn't in my homelands of England at the time and was involved in a situation that was very difficult. One day, I was praying for guidance to the Divine. Instead, my prayers were answered by someone entirely different: the old mermaids of Albion.

In a spirit vision I was taken across a wild, gray sea that was so familiar to me it felt the same as the blood flowing through my veins; it was the North Sea on the north coast of England in Yorkshire where I was born. Mermaids were swirling on the winds and in the frothy tips of the thrashing waves and escorting me into a cave. Inside the sea cave, the mermaids infused me with a sea spray of wisdom from their ancient folk, giving me an energy transmission. It felt as if a salty flood from those wild, magical, ferocious seas had passed right through into my DNA. Afterward, there was a knowing in me that I couldn't explain but felt like a homecoming.

Later on, with some research, I discovered there were numerous legends of mermaids in the caves at Flamborough Head, where I had been taken in my spirit vision, and that local folklore says that at nearby Runswick Bay, also by the North Sea, women would carry their children into a cave at night for cures, believing that a powerful spirit inhabited the womblike cave. So the ancestors were calling me back home, not just in a physical sense but in a deeper sense, calling me back into the stories in my body, in my bones, in my blood, in my womb, and in my lineage.

I also reconnected to the magical Cloud End in the northwest of England, a place where the veils were thin and that was once sacred to the witches and wizards of the old ways of magic. In the dream time, the word *awen* was imprinting on my consciousness, and so I began my apprenticeship into the path of awen. This involved many adventures, including a rebirth ceremony in a quoit (a megalithic stone chamber that consists of standing stones capped by a large stone) on the Welsh borderlands with a wily witch lady; a communion with the sacred lands of Saveock in Cornwall—home to a sacred healing spring and the legacy of the swan priestesses dedicated to the goddess Bride or Brighid; and a deepening of my relationship with the sacred lands of Avalon in Glastonbury, home of the Lady of the Lake, and the holy island of Iona in the Hebrides in Scotland, known as the isle of druids and once home to a famous witch oracle (like the oracle of Delphi), whom kings visited to take counsel and prophecy from.

Over time, life and the land were weaving my spirit back into wholeness, and I was remembering something long forgotten and fragile as an early morning glittering in a spider's web, unseen but now illuminated by a rising sun, so that I could see the threads, the web nodes, the weave.

The ancestors were asking me to become an *awenydd*—a Brythonic word for a native British spirit keeper of the lands. The tradition of awen is one of inspiration, spirit, receiving energy, and weaving it back into the world. Awen is the flowing feminine energy spirit that infuses all the living creation, both seen and unseen. It's the juice of creation, most abundant in a woman's womb, that creates life. It is shakti, anima, magic, enchantment, kundalini, and the Holy Spirit. An awenydd—a spirit keeper—is a weaver of stories from the feminine energy magic, from Mother Earth, and a chalice that channels the rays of wisdom flowing from the cosmic Womb.

Mam Tor, Home of the Ancestors

Sitting at the heart of these essays I share with you is the story of my personal ancestral lineage at Mam Tor (Mother Mountain), in the Peak District of the Old North of England, once the grail lands of Maid Marian and Robin Hood and the ancient tribe of the Brigantes—who worshipped the goddess Brigantia, the ancient mother of the old north—who were once led by powerful queens. These lands are an ancestral soulmate within me, the earth placenta of my childhood.

I have planted the bodies of both of my parents in the foothills of Mam Tor, in the magical Hope Valley. This old ceremonial land is humming with the traditions of the old ways and is populated by witch stones, menhirs, bride stones, and old caves once inhabited by our Neanderthal kin, who also live on within our genetic memory, speaking to us of a time before this time began.

One rainy night in August back in 2016, during a visit to Castleton—a beautiful little village with a castle on the hill and Mam Tor and Winnats Pass looming over it—the ancestors beckoned me to tell their tales again. The dragon spirit in Mam Tor was awakening, they told me, and they wanted me to get busy with some spirit weaving on her behalf. Over three intense days in a very small cottage, I furiously scribed the essay, often early in the morning, late at night, or even in the middle of the night as the ancestors woke me. My husband, Azra, and coauthor of my previous books was also with me, also feeling the pulsing, intense magic coming from the mountain, as if the ancestors were visibly walking among us.

Wherever you are in the world, and whatever land lineage you are from, the ancestors wish for this wild magic to be shared, and for everyone to have a seat at this table, to drink this awen.

I felt that the ancestors were making me a home in the foothills of the spirit worlds they inhabited so that I could weave energy across the worlds. They also reminded me of the importance of *village news*: it's a very ordinary kind of spirit weaving, very old, very feminine, which in their estimation is the most important kind of spirit work to do right now. Village news is the ordinary, practical magic that weaves our communities together with care, connection, festivities, feasting, celebrations, grief rituals, blessingways, birth passageways, and a general sense of knowing what's up with everyone else around you, including the nonhuman neighbors. It's not gossip, nosiness, or prying; it's that care that reaches out and says, "Are you all right, love?" and let's everyone know what's going on so that we understand one another's lives and challenges. It's the feminine magic that knows we are all entangled and connected together.

It's like grannies in a knitting circle, or the fisherman's wives mending nets together, or mothers weaving and sewing with their sisters to create magical garments for their children. It's homespun magic, and it's so powerful it just went right ahead and created the known world.

Village News, Feminine Magic

It reminds me of the magic of my childhood, which was so deeply embedded I barely noticed it, as it seeped right into the flesh and blood of my being. When I was little, my mum held coffee mornings at her house, where all the women gathered in the front room. This wasn't a superficial suburban gathering just for idle gossip (though there could be plenty of that!), it was also a women's community circle of important village news.

Women thick with age, sorrow and experience, bawdy laughs, and faces that could collapse into new shapes with sympathy took seats wherever they could and allowed themselves to relax, shoulders slumped a little, tan tights wrinkled, into a world where they felt safe to just be.

Of course, no one actually drank coffee. This was Yorkshire, and the only acceptable beverage was strong tea. For two hours the kettle boiled and roiled like it was a bubbling cauldron. When I was very young, I wasn't allowed into the meeting and instead sat behind the closed door with my ear pressed tightly against it, listening and catching drifts of village news. They talked about things that were taboo in normal life: death, sickness, babies, sex, struggling marriages, money woes, thrifty bargains, children and family, and even supernatural stuff.

As I got older, I was allowed to make the tea and come into the room to serve it with plates of cheap biscuits from the supermarket, such as digestives, ginger nuts, and rich tea biscuits.

Eventually at eight years old, wearing a grown-up skirt and shoes with little cork heels, I was allowed to attend, as everyone cooed "ooh isn't she grown up," and I sat at the feet of my mum, who occupied the prime position of the golden velour armchair, and listened with wonder.

Now, as I've grown older, I understand some of those conversations in a deeper way that back then flew over my head but managed to land in my subconscious like a fluttering raven. They were right to wait until I was eight to enter that woman's world of village news, because some of what I heard frightened and unsettled me, because it seemed the world was bigger, weirder, scarier, more supernatural, full of more suffering and strange joys than I could have imagined.

Suburban Shamans, Ordinary Oracles

Yorkshire was famous for its weird and wild magic, with the legendary Yorkshire Witch and folktales of shape-shifting cunning women and a fire-breathing dragon who was tamed by local women's home-baked parkin (a type of sticky cake), alongside legends of enchanted wells, haunted henges, ancient barrows, vampires, aliens, a famous meteor, and the otherworldly leylines of the Yorkshire Wolds and its Gypsey Race River, which is associated with prophecy.

Yorkshire still has many traces of goddess worship, from Sheela-na-gigs on churches to the altar stone of a snake goddess, holding two serpents, one in each hand, connected to a river. The land was understood to be made of dragon energy, and folktales told of how Filey Brig, which I visited with my parents for many years, was once a living dragon who turned to stone.

The women in my mum's circle were like the Hen Wives of old, knowing and bawdy, with not an ounce of puritanism in them. They felt free to cackle over a cuppa and talk frankly about sex; and the "hen nights" in the local area were famous for drunken female revelry and debauchery.

Magic for these women was ordinary, and it didn't happen with fancy or fanfare, but they believed in it, even if they wouldn't have consciously articulated it. In fact, if you had asked them about magic, they would have laughed at you for being daft. But it was still there.

The big village news that rocked my early childhood was about the local well. We had an old well on a spare piece of land in our tight-knit little cul-de-sac of a community that was mostly forgotten by people. The land itself was high up on a hill with views out all across the moors and hills and was named for sacred springs and may well have been an ancient sacred place to our ancestors, many, many moons ago. The spirit of place is a persistent being with a long memory.

When I was six, the news (which I heard through the door and which frightened the bejesus out of me) was that the household of my little best friend, also six years old, was having problems with a poltergeist. Long descriptions of the poltergeist activity were given. The women clucked with the supernatural audacity of it all, and the nuisance of spirits in your kitchen cupboards.

A local psychic woman, renowned for her clairvoyance and ability to negotiate with spirits, was called out. Looking on these small, drab working-class homes of northern suburbs in the '70s, it might be difficult to imagine we had women doing the work that we now call shamanism. But they were. Often in very humble and straightforward ways, as a form of community service.

I had heard about psychics before, spoken of with hushed and respectful tones. My mum's mum was one of ten children, and she had many sisters who lived close by her all her life. These women gathered every night, leaving the menfolk, for village news meetings, and their main guidance in life was taken from local psychic women, not male priests or spiritual counselors.

The female psychics operated from their own homes, often small terrace houses or council houses, and they worked entirely from word of mouth in the female community. From what my mum said, the men rarely visited these psychics and saw it more as silly women's superstition.

Mum recounted, with horror and awe, her meeting with one of these psychics when she was a young woman. Her auntie (one of the sisters) had taken her along to a session. Mum said it was just an ordinary terrace house, and they sat in the front living room with other women to wait for their time slot. The psychic lady saw people in her back bedroom. The psychic had said that Mum would marry someone with the initials AA soon (she married my dad a few years later, who had the initials AA). She gave Auntie her money back saying that it was strange but she couldn't see anything in the future for her. A few weeks later Mum's auntie died unexpectedly.

This memory stuck with my mum, and she was respectful of, and also terrified of, psychic women. So the news that our neighbor had called upon a psychic for a home visit, of all things, was really big news. It was like the pope popping round to give you a blessing. Except it wasn't male ordained. It revealed a hidden woman's world of nonrational magic bubbling away.

 Well Blessings, Ancient Curses

As it turned out, it was more of an exorcism. The psychic said that spirits were coming up through the well, and this was the source of the poltergeist activity. My friends and I often played around this well, and indeed it did have a very strange and unsettling energy, most likely because it had been abandoned as a source of wisdom and nourishment for the community.

On the say so of the psychic, my best friend's mum actually sold her house and moved away from the area, so great was her fear of the troubled well. Many years later, in my teens, a wealthy developer built his own home on this piece of land, right on top of the troubled well. This was bad news because for him as a modern man of money operating in a modern scientific rational world, this was a prime piece of real estate, and local legends were silly nonsense.

Shortly afterward, his young daughter died tragically, and it prompted a spell of strange deaths in our community, from teenagers to people in their early forties dying in their sleep. Village news meetings were convened with furious and frightened talk. Some of the women said that the property developer had brought a curse on the land, and they worried about who would be next. Growing up to be a modern woman, I thought that this was probably a bit of crazy talk.

But at night in bed, my consciousness would travel to the well trapped under the rich man's house, built without care or consideration for the sacred landscape. And I could feel the trapped, troubled energy of a beautiful sacred well, now forgotten, blocked, and "damned" up. I could hear spirit voices of the ancestors drifting up from that well, and they weren't the happy ancestors; they were the trapped spirits who had become lost when we'd forgotten the land.

As the women in the suburbs were contemplating the problems of a cursed well, a beloved female relative was actively tending to a sacred well so that it might bless her community.

One of my aunties, whom we often visited, lived outside the suburbs and near the sacred lands of Mam Tor on a farm, in a rural village. She was a Spirit Keeper of the Well for her community, one of the village "church" women who participated in the annual well dressing ceremonies.

These rituals were rooted right back into ancient Goddess worship, where a well was considered to be the sacred vulva of the Goddess and the entryway to the Underworld and Otherworld. It was a portal between worlds, in the

*My auntie Margaret (top left-hand side), as a maiden of honor to
the May Queen in the May Day (Beltane) celebrations in
Hope Valley, Peak District, in the 1950s*

same way a women's womb is a portal between the worlds. It was also a living grail or chalice. To block up, neglect, or build over a well or springs was considered to bring bad fortune and made the faerie folk angry and vengeful.

My visits to the farm, and the crafts my auntie taught me, were a light of inspiration in my childhood, speaking of beauty, care, and tradition. Little did I know the symbolism of these well dressings, honoring the feminine portals into Earth, would become the guiding mythology of my life.

When the well of the feminine is tended and celebrated, adorned with flowers, acknowledged, cherished, and loved, the world blooms with feminine magic, abundance, and creativity. When the wells are blocked or harmed, a curse comes upon the land, and the world becomes infertile.

At the root of feminine magic are women's mysteries—the Womb

Well dressing at Malvern, Welsh Borders, United Kingdom

Mysteries—the taboo wisdom that grows in cycles and sheds blood and keens its ecstasies and griefs, that weaves and births life, that tends to death and whispers incantations to the new shoots of rebirth.

Women naturally hold this magic deep in their womb space, and all people hold this spiritual womb energy. We are all born from the deep feminine womb, and all of us are children of the moon. Feminine energy belongs to everyone, and we all have a "feminine well" inside.

This is the spirit of wisdom in which I offer these essays to you, celebrating the power of ordinary women's magic and the feminine spirit that inhabits all living things. It is time now that we tend the wells again, return to our simple, humble hearth magic, and re-create our world.

Truth is, I've got the kettle on, with an offering of tasty cookies on a plate, and I'm inviting you in to reconvene the village news meetings, where we gather together and share our wisdom.

Like those old village news meetings I remember, this book of essays is intended to feel like being inside a cozy, warm living room, listening to fragments of conversations, occasional long stories, love notes, coos of encouragement, the odd bemoaning, and those treasured moments when we sit together in comfortable silence that feels like a big, soft old couch.

Take everything I say with a pinch of salt, and only take home whatever feels helpful and true.

WELL WISHES,
SEREN BERTRAND,
VALENTINE'S DAY

SPINNING
OUR WEB

ONE

SPIRIT WEAVING

Path of Feminine Magic

Spirit weaving is a feminine magic that brings threads together into a complex, beautiful whole—creating a pattern that brings deep wisdom and encodes the very secrets of life.

According to the dictionary, *weaving* means "to interlace the threads of the warp and weft" or "to interweave elements into a complex whole." Feminine magic is not about transcending, leaving, ascending, or detaching—it is about *weaving*, bringing different threads together.

Spirit weavers are mistresses of duality, bringing diverse threads into a mystical tapestry that is filled with love, beauty, divine pattern, creative flair, innovation, imagination, and celebration.

Since time out of mind, women's magic has been encoded by the humble feminine arts of weaving, spinning, stitching, sewing, and knitting together. It has also been known as the red thread—the menstrual magic passed down from the primordial womb of the ancient mothers. It was thought that women wove, knitted, and stitched babies into being inside their wombs.

This was known as the distaff path of feminine spirituality, a tradition that has been passed down since prehistoric times, often by mothers and daughters or communities of magicians and wise women dedicated to the innate magic of the spirit of Mother Earth and the cosmic mothers—the great weavers who wove us into being and who placed divine threads of love deep inside us.

The distaff path refers to the feminine arts, and anything on the left-hand side of creation. It also refers to the mother's line of descent in the family, the matriarchal legacy and lineage. The earliest use of *distaff* in English also refers to a spinning implement: a long stick used for spinning flax or wool or other fibers. From this, the distaff came to represent women or women's work. This was the original feminine magic wand, with powers of alchemy and transformation.

In fairy tales we often hear about spinning and weaving as magical pursuits, stories that veil teachings about spiritual initiation, especially for young women at their coming of age.

Goddesses are also spirit weavers, and the Norns and Fates also spin and weave destiny.

Spinning and weaving also refers to time magic—spinning time—and time is the grandmother of life and death. Even more powerful than death herself is the spinner and weaver of time who brings patterns into being and unravels them again. The time weaver or spirit weaver creates and unpicks life. This is connected to women's magic as soul doulas, who stand at the threshold of life and death and whose songs of the Otherworld accompany new and departing souls.

This tradition of spirit weaving is ancient and found across the world. In nearly all shrines dedicated to Artemis, spindle whorls, loom weights, and shuttles have been found, and in her sanctuaries, woolen clothing and threads wound on spools were offered as gifts to her. On Corinthian vases, Artemis and her womb priestesses are seen holding a spindle.

The Sami goddess Beiwe was linked to spinning and flax, and offerings of spinning wheels were made during sacred festivals. In Baltic traditions the sun goddess Saule had a spinning wheel that spun sunrays. Moon goddesses, such as Kuutar in Finland, were often spinners who made magical garments from moonlight. The Slavic goddess Mokosh was in charge of women's destiny and spinning and weaving, and people prayed to Mokosh stones—breast-shaped boulders. In Russia a spinning device called a *prialka* was placed in cribs, and women made marriages at winter spinning gatherings.

The Native American Spider Woman is also a spinner who teaches the magic of weaving, and the goddess Ixchel in the Mayan lands of Mexico is a lunar goddess associated with weaving.

In older times in England, the goddess Arianhrod—she of the spinning silver wheel—was the matroness of flax, and women would show their vulva to the flax in the fields to make it grow.

Ancient taboos around spinning and weaving are connected to protections for women and allow women to have special days off for the Goddess and time off from work during pregnancy.

Spinning and weaving was the ancient code for women's work—women's feminine magic.

Women would gather in small groups and circles, sharing eucharists of herbal tea, village news, and pregnant silence as they crafted clothes and blankets for their family and community. They often sewed magical symbols, such as the elemental cruciform, into talismanic clothes or blankets that were bound in spells and energies of protection, especially for children and marriages. Special blankets were crafted for children, and they would sleep under a handmade layer of embroidered and stitched protection that also spelled out the secrets of the universe.

Quilt patterns such as grandmother's garden contain complex sacred geometries that encoded secrets of the structure of creation and how the Great Galactic Mother wove Mother Earth and all her creatures from inside her Womb. These secret feminine teachings were passed down in heirloom patterns and geometries sewn into quilts and stitched into symbols on special clothes. Sacred quilts or blankets were even crafted as homespun shrouds for the beloved deceased.

Witchcraft used knitting, sewing, spinning, and weaving to cast spells and weather-weave. Witches in Cornwall stitched with special glass knitting needles as they made incantations. Often knitting spells were unraveled afterward, dissolved like the sand mandalas of Eastern tradition.

The path of feminine magic is the path of the householder and the housewife, who is the true alchemist who spins and creates life and worlds. Often in secret with no praise or remuneration.

 ## Crafty Magic
Weaving a World

When I was growing up and reading tales, lore, and myth, the heroes were always men leaving home, off to do something important, and even the heroine princess ended up escaping from the palace, or from the tower where she was spinning gold. Housewives weren't heroic. In fact, you rarely ever read about what it takes to live a daily life: to tend your garden, grow your food, rear animals, build and maintain a house, clean, prepare and cook food, raise children, and keep in good relations with yourself, the greater family, the village, and the larger community.

And you certainly never read or heard about the secret magic of *domestic witchery*—despite the fact that fairy tales were filled with witches stirring cauldrons over the stove or growing herbs, and that most magical fairy lore was set in the domestic realm and featured domestic duties.

Over time, I began to realize that I was looking far, far away for magical alchemists when all I had to do was look down at the place my feet were planted and the alembics of my own pots. In feminine magical tradition your home and body are the magnetic center that grows your power.

Many moons ago, I was commissioned by a major newspaper in England to write a story about the changing face of housewifery over the past century. I had pitched the idea to them; meanwhile, I was the archnemesis of the housewife in my own life, renowned for cooking food that could maim or kill and only able to forage or identify food from my favorite restaurant menus in London. I had vowed to never get married and worshipped vintage stiletto boots.

In my early thirties, I was starting my "return": like a ball of thread, I had tossed myself bravely out into the world to escape the realm of my childhood, but now that red thread was starting to reel me back in, tugging on my womb, reminding me of the power of *coming home*.

So I got on a train and set off back home to Yorkshire to talk to the local ladies. My mum had arranged an interview with a woman who was then in her nineties and had been newly married in the 1940s. I had presumed this would be a private interview, but when I arrived home, the whole tribe was in my mum's living room, ready for the grand event. It was one of the most humbling and enlightening moments of my life, to hear this elderly lady share the secrets of her earlier life.

What I heard inspired me. As a young married woman in her twenties, moving into her first home without her parents, she had made, crafted, and created *everything*. She told me how she had sewn the curtains and tablecloths, pegged the rugs for the floor, and even crafted paper flowers, placed in a glass vase made from an old bottle to adorn the table. I was familiar with homespun magic. My own mum had sewn all our curtains and bedspreads and handmade the lampshades, and together we had collected shells from the beach on my holiday, to stick onto wine bottles to make lamp stands. My mum even once handmade our kitchen cupboards from wood. But my mum's thriftiness came from financial necessity, and as soon as she could afford it, she hit the shops for modern mass-produced goods. But the older lady had bought only the very basics, and the rest was left to her own creativity, craftiness, and imagination.

She also told me a touching story about her patchwork wedding dress. At that time everything was on ration, including lace and silk. She couldn't afford a wedding dress, so the entire community donated their rations of one small square piece of silk. She stitched each patch of the neighborhood's generous fabric donation into her patchwork wedding dress, weaving true magic.

How have we lost and devalued these feminine arts of crafting and creating? In just a few generations, these old traditions of crafting, weaving, spinning, sewing are almost gone.

In Victorian times, women were so crafty that they wore chatelaines, a kind of magic witch's belt. This special feminine belt was worn around their waist holding their magical tools—small knives, needles, scissors—so they could be prepared for any small repair in the household.

Of course, hand-making things is a lot of hard work—but it also contains *immense magic*. When we craft or create something we infuse it with spells of intention. It becomes *ensouled*. If we mend something, it brings us into the power of *repair*, where we regenerate and heal that which has broken. It helps us move away from thinking that life is disposable or easily replaced.

When we craft something with our own hands, we infuse it with our creative womb power and feminine magic, and if we do this ritually and with intention, we step into the distaff lineage of the spirit weavers of witchcraft. We start to become initiated into the powers of creation.

And when we have immersed in these feminine arts of domestic witchery, we can apply them to even deeper acts of quantum magic, as we are now in embodied resonance with the Creatrix.

Words can also be woven together, like spells, and come from the tips of our tongue or the tips of our fingers. They are spirit power that is becoming embodied, which is a spirit weave.

Recently, a friend shared a dream she'd had about me. She had seen me in a house with needles and threads everywhere: pin cushions hung from the ceiling in every room and threads dangled down from the Upperworld, as if everywhere I went, I was weaving threads together.

I felt so inspired by her dream, and what a beautiful vision it was of being on the feminine path.

The red thread is the feminine wisdom passed through the matriarchal line, stitching generations of witches together since time immemorial, as if held on a great thread hung with lanterns of knowledge and shared experience. We often talk about telling a good yarn, having money-spinning ideas, or spinning a tale. Spinsters were single unmarried women who often made their living spinning and may have also practiced other magical feminine arts for their community. In Basque traditions, the home was considered to be the church, and firesides were the altars.

Symbolism of the red thread was a very real practice in feminine magic. Tying a red thread around trees or wands or wearing it on the wrist represents the magical protection and blessings of the ancient mothers who watch over us. In faerie tradition the Rowan tree—*the red tree*—is associated with feminine magic, and people tied red threads around a twig of rowan and carried it around with them for protection and healing, as a kind of feminine ancestral wand.

For our wedding in Wales we tied a large red ribbon around a grove of trees and got married inside the faerie circle it created. Afterward, in a beautiful round house, to the sounds of harp, the bard who married us incanted the Prophecy of Merlin. Our union was woven together by the red thread of the ancestral magical blessing.

Across time this red thread of legacy is associated with the motherline, home, hearth, and *humble magic*—the kind of feminine magic that is empowered by the earth and the deep ancestors.

The deep alchemy of our times is for us to awaken our *feminine magic*—to quantum leap from housewife into *housewitch* and magic weaver, tending the hearthside feminine churches. A home is wherever we live, whatever we love or tend, whatever supports, shelters, and nourishes us. No matter what our gender or work status, our home is our quantum womb and cathedral. Ultimately, our body is the most foundational home we have, inside the greater home of Earth.

Home is a powerful metaphor for a true center, a birthing place, and a destination we return to.

Housewifery at its most secret heart is the loving tending of our Mother Earth and all of life. The secret truth of every tradition is that the greatest alchemists were always the housewives. Unnamed, silent, secret, spinning magic worlds across time. Weaving life together.

And don't be fooled by how simple it sounds. Feminine magic births entire universes.

Maiden of the Rainbow

Pohyola's fair and winsome daughter,
Glory of the land and water,
Sat upon the bow of heaven,
On its highest arch resplendent,
In a gown of richest fabric,
In a gold and silver air-gown,
Weaving webs of golden texture,
Interlacing threads of silver,
Weaving with a golden shuttle,
With a weaving-comb of silver;
Merrily flies the golden shuttle,
From the maiden's nimble fingers,
Briskly swings the lathe in weaving,
Swiftly flies the comb of silver,
From the sky-born maiden's fingers,
Weaving webs of wondrous beauty.

FROM RUNE VIII, *THE KALEVALA*

BY ELIAS LONNROT

TWO

FEMININE POWER

Awaken Your Spiritual Womb

We are living through intense times, and we need support. The idea we can do it all alone is a thoughtform of separation. Yet with everyone else in the same chaotic world, dealing with their own stuff, how can we access this unconditional support we crave without making unrealistic demands on others?

The answer lives within our spiritual Womb, a *homeplace* inside us—a place that lives deep within us but is far vaster than us and holds the primordial energy of love that birthed us.

We all have a spiritual Womb—whether we are male or female. In a woman, this is located in the area of her physical uterus. In a man, it is located under the navel, sometimes called the hara.

We can feel this spiritual Womb as an inner divine mother, or the immanent presence of God, which has been called Sophia, Shekinah, or the feminine Holy Grail.

By accessing this reservoir of infinite supportive energy, we can begin to go beyond our limited stories and the reactive emotions generated by our traumatized pain-body. We can find that doorway of rebirth within our own being. We become a mother to ourselves, and to our entire lineage. This connection begins to weave magical possibilities that manifest for us in direct and incredibly synchronistic ways. We begin to trust that life truly does support us.

How Do We Access This Inner Spiritual Womb?

The gateway to this magical well of support is within our deep body consciousness.

Often when we're feeling stressed, triggered and traumatized, we come out of our body. We also disconnect from our pelvis and core, which is our inner throne.

We tense, tighten, ascend into the mind, and leave our deep inner wisdom and the vast ocean of primordial creative energy that lives within our spiritual Womb.

The healing is to descend down into our spiritual Womb on an umbilical cord of light, to breathe, to feel, to reconnect, and to discover the ocean of energy within.

A feminine sense of enlightenment is to fully relax into the body.

Our body and psyche contract through fear, pain, and old patterns. This holding or tension becomes the obstacle or boulder that blocks the flow of life or light.

These psychic and physical tensions, usually interwoven, are caused by trauma—either a one-off big shock or, more likely, repetitive bite-sized trauma, originating since our time in the womb and then gathering layers like a slow-rolling snowball.

What Is the Magic Doorway to Healing?

When we can soften and relax these long-standing tension patterns, the light bulb switches on as the body and soul open like a flower and are bathed in light essence. We can soften this pain-body through many methods—bodywork, therapy, prayer, ceremony, and many other healing methods—but often the relief is only temporary. Once the treatment or therapy is over, the pain contracts in on itself again, like a hedgehog curling into a ball and guarding itself with protective spikes.

It's easy to say to ourselves or to others "just relax" or "let go"—but it's a magical act of deep soul alchemy to actually take that inner psychic skydive. When we do, we can transform ourselves in a lasting way, creating a dimensional shift in our lives.

But first we have to meet the inner place that is stuck in trauma or tension—and we also have to connect with the spiritual Womb that can hold these feelings in safety and wisdom.

The wounded inner child, who once held on for dear life to survive, equates letting go with danger and disaster. On a deeply subconscious level, this place tells us that:

> To hold on or tighten equals survival.
> To let go or soften equals death.

Sometimes people flip-flop between both poles—going from control to chaos. Some polarize into rigid control. Some fall apart into a living disaster zone.

Every time we choose to rigidly control our life, we lock out the flow of love. Every time we let go into trauma, we add another layer of pain to the snowball.

We have to let go into the Womb of love who birthed us and who can catch us.

Our healing can never come from more fragmentation or from fracturing ourselves time and time again. This is why "crazy" wisdom paths based on traumatic initiations or aggressive and confrontational truth rarely lead to long-lasting psychic healing. Our healing comes from restoration and the holistic, tender reweaving of our heart. When we have had our heart broken, opening can bring that fracture line into acute awareness again. This thread of pain and grief can be included in the tapestry of love as our heart opens again, bringing with it an immense experience of orgasmic grieving, where our deepest wounds are freshly bathed in expansive love.

Deep breaths . . . let go, let Goddess.
Healing happens when we trust and let go into this inner Womb of love.

Where we feel ourselves holding tight, either physically or psychically, we can soften and let go into the immense holding container of this universal Womb. We let go into something greater than us that can hold *all* of our feelings.

Take a pause for a moment:

𝒟 Imagine letting go into a huge energy of support that will always catch you.

𝒟 Visualize yourself free-falling into an infinite black velvet Womb of love.

𝒟 Allow a wave of softness to wash through your body and your heart.

Be playful, imagine it as a dark shimmering night sky lining your womb with magical stars or a big orange bouncy castle or warm arms—whatever makes you feel held.

This feminine holding presence created everything, knows everything, and is connected to everything. It knows exactly what you need, and knows the way forward for you. You can trust this spiritual Womb completely.

When we let go into this incredible holding container, we experience the flow of the universe rush back into us. We enter a zone that brings wholeness and renewal. From this place, finally, we can begin to heal, transform, and alchemize our pain.

 ## Field of Collective Grace

In old gnostic lore it was said that the adversary energy—a negative force that created suffering in the world—was a greater-than-human intelligence. The gnostic sages told how it was impossible to face this energy from our limited personal self.

To face this powerful adversary, people needed to call on the power of grace—the infinite intelligence of love that was large enough to face and rebirth this adversary.

This greater-than-human intelligence that sabotages us can also be expressed as a massive collective wound-field. This energy is filled with the subconscious pain of our own lives and past lives, of our ancestors' lives, and of the mysterious hidden memories of the collective pain-body of the world going back to the dawn of time.

It feels like an impossible task to take in and transmute the immensity of this pain.

What is needed is to call upon and tune into the collective grace-field, to awaken ourselves into the great field of the spiritual Womb, which connects us together and brings us into the primordial grace of life herself.

Spiritual Womb Ritual

〗 Make, reuse, or buy a purse or string-tied pouch to symbolize the Womb.

〗 Have a stash of thin strips of paper ready to write on.

〗 Every night before you go to bed, write a worry down.

〗 Put it into your Womb pouch. Imagine that the Womb of love is holding it.

〗 At the end of thirty days (or a lunar cycle, ideally the dark moon), bring all these slips out and observe all your worry words.

〗 Notice how many worries have resolved or feel less daunting.

〗 Burn the worry words in a small pot with the following incantation:

> *Worry, worry, the world's still spinning,*
> *Worry, worry, love's still winning.*
> *Worry, worry, bless your heart,*
> *Worry, worry, it's time for us to part.*
> *Well, Well, Well. All is well.*

THREE

WOMB REVOLUTION

Women's Body Magic

One of the deepest secrets is that the body of woman, especially the womb and the landscape of the feminine soul, is intimately entwined with the fate of Mother Earth.

As the rivers of Earth have been polluted and Earth pillaged, so has the feminine soul and the body of woman been desecrated—through both subtle and overt abuse.

The fate of our world now lives in the bodies of women. Earth is calling women to awaken within their female bodies. Earth is calling us to awaken our wombs and reclaim our magical birthing powers and the mystical dark moon powers of rebirth. This reclamation is an epic pilgrimage of sheer courage: it takes us along the darkest pathways our modern culture has led us down to find our way back to the light of our own power and our organic true nature.

Earth is also calling for men and the masculine energy to become Guardians of the Feminine, to awaken their own feminine soul, and to dismantle their inner psychic conditioning. With this, an entirely new species of man and masculine energy is being birthed: the Son and Lover of the Goddess. As men remember this guardianship, the immense, fertile, raw power of Mother Earth comes to enthrone them, gifting them the greening power of creation.

Earth is asking us to rebirth the sensual powers of the awakened woman. Earth is asking us to rebirth the heart-wealth of the awakened man.

Spirit Weaving Wisdom

Here are some keys to a womb-centered revolution:

☽ Prioritize the health and well-being of your physical body.

☽ Prioritize the joy and inspiration of your heart and soul.

☽ Breathe into your womb or *hara* (beneath the navel) for ten minutes a day.

☽ Listen to the intuitive womb voice within your body consciousness.

☽ Follow your instincts even when your logical mind disagrees.

☽ Allow yourself to rest and to not always be doing or productive.

☽ Find ways to experience more pleasure, enjoyment, and sensuality.

☽ Vision your sexual energy and sexual desire as something holy.

☽ Be truthful with your feelings and ask for what you need.

☽ Dare to share your deep feminine essence with a trusted lover.

☽ Shine bright and be a wild light of feminine wisdom in the world.

Cosmic Birth

Dragon Priestesses of Earth

We need to remember how to hold the line. We need to hold the vision.

In the dream time, I am visited by magical spirit horses, vibrating with pulsing life power, surrounded by spots of shimmering light, like luminous cosmic polka dots.

These are the spirit horses from the caves of Peche Merle in the Midi Pyrenees, France.

They carry and gallop a message to me from the ancestral womb shamans to follow the horse tracks, the sacred paths, the faerie ways of feminine earth consciousness.

Earth spirit, the soul of the world, is singing to me—calling, shouting. I hear this beauty song, this anguished cry, reverberating across filaments of light that weave across the world in a web of energy, flowering at sacred sites, our earthly temples.

The gateway-time is at hand.
We are on *red alert*.
Yet red is the color of our womb blood,
It holds our sacred birthing power.
It holds our wisdom memory,
In an unbroken genetic line,
Back to the Ancient Mothers.
We need to hold the line.

During a Vision of Magdalene I see her lineage:

She leads me to a low-built hut, and I lean over to enter the door-birth-canal. Inside there is a coven of Magdalene priestesses, naked except for diaphanous red veils that fall like water across the curves of their bodies. The women are orgasmically offering their moon blood to the holy center, the red power of potential impregnating their deepest prayers of love and creative possibility. They are breathing with the magnetic pulse of Earth, their wombs at one with the great Womb of the Mother, their intentions imbued with a sacred birthing magic. The collective power of their dreams, prayers, and intentions—seeded within the primordial fertility of their sacred blood—is gathering potency, distilling futures from the cauldron of Mother Earth's Womb, redreaming the past, and building bridges to the future, for women to cross over and remember, when the time is ripe.

We need to remember the lineage and to redream the lines.

Leila Castle says in her anthology of women at sacred sites:

I had a vision of a very black-skinned Aboriginal man standing in the sun-baked Australian desert. He was naked except for a loincloth and leaned on a wooden staff. He didn't speak, but in my mind I understood his words very clearly: "You people aren't holding your lines there." It was like an admonishment and warning that the invisible threads of a planetary web of interconnections—what the Aboriginal people call the songlines—had been dropped by our culture.

We must hold the energy lines of the Earth grid.
We are holding and weaving the universe together.
We must keep going, visioning the energy web of Earth's body.
We must keep connecting to the vibrating hum of the ley lines.
We must protect the dragon lines of Earth's birth chakras.

Standing strong as rock,
Rivers flowing through our hearts.
We sing your song.
We hold the line.

Our ancestral line is also calling for remembrance.
We must find the forgotten faerie paths in our bodies.
We must awaken the songlines of the Womb.
The Womb is the temple of Earth's song.
The Womb of woman must start singing in tune with Earth again.
Our sexual energy and birthing power must root into the Womb of Gaia.
It is time to awaken our Womb sovereignty and plant our power deep.
It is time to rewild the Womb and rebirth the world.

We must also hold the celestial lines too.
Our ancestors danced with the stars.
We must remember the astrological waltz.
We must find our cosmic rhythm again.
We must birth stargates through our Womb.
The fate of our universe depends on it.

I am reminded of Philip Pullman's gnostic epic *His Dark Materials*—more aptly called "Her Dark Materials." In this symbolic story, an invisible elementary particle called Dust, which communicates through the alethiometer, is the magical secret substance at the root of the world's mysteries. This mystical Dust—a fictional version of dark matter—is unique because it is conscious and is also formed when matter becomes conscious. A religious institution, which dominates the world, has decreed Dust as the Original Sin and is set on destroying the consciousness of matter—the Dark Mother field. This sacred substance is draining out of all worlds at an alarming rate, and only the power of true love can reenchant the multiverse.

Pray with Your Soul Fire

We must not give up—
Even though birth pangs have us howling
Crowning a new consciousness
Now is the time to dream harder
Sing louder
Dance further

Pray with your soul fire
Be bold, summon your power
Dare fate with radical acts of beauty
Keep weaving, keep weaving,
Keep holding the lines
The ancestors are with us
The earth ancestors are supporting us
The celestial ancestors are guiding us
Find your place in the web, find your node, find your note
Hold your place in the web with fierce love and courage
When enough of us hold the songlines strong
A new tune will birth, a new song,
Through the Womb of Mother Earth
Earth will sing itself into a new cycle
She will sing through you.

We must restore our Womb sovereignty and reconnect our sexuality with Earth. This is our *power*. Our birthing essence belongs to the web of life; it cannot be owned, bought, stolen, possessed, commoditized—or even disowned or destroyed. It is the source of who we are; it is the golden serpent of consciousness within matter.

Root down, rise up, flower open.
Grow wild.
It is time.

Resources

Castle, Leila. *Earthwalking Sky Dancers: Women's Pilgrimages to Sacred Places.* Berkeley: Frog Books/North Atlantic Books, 1996.

Pullman, Philip. *His Dark Materials (Trilogy).* New York: Knopf, 1996.

FIVE

MOON MYSTERIES

Lunar Cycles of Wisdom

Throughout our lives there is a silent witness to all our joys, our pains, our wildest longings, and our deepest grief. The moon is there with us, shining her essence into the waterways of our body and soul, so we may never be alone.

Every 29.5 days the moon completes her orbit around Earth, showing us the magical phases of her feminine faces: the bright maiden of her crescent new moon, the shining mother of her full moon, and the wise crone of her dark moon.

She holds the mystical power of conception, gestation, birth, and rebirth. She renews herself in magical cycles of creativity, marrying dark to light. She is the mistress of alchemy and the cup bearer of compassion.

The cellular structure of water changes and transforms with moonlight.

We are mermaids, made up of almost 70 percent water, and so the moon also transforms us. In ancient times, indigenous people and female womb shamans worked with this mystical, transformative power of the moon—to help them seed and birth creations.

They followed the turning wheel of the moon's phases and lived by her time.

Now we are being called to remember this feminine shamanic path and become har-moon-ious with the sacred rhythms of life again. To awaken as moon priestesses.

When we consciously work with the power of the moon, we become lunar alchemists. The moon is waiting to whisper her forgotten secrets to you.

As the sun sets on the seen world, make friends with the darkened unseen world.

Follow the sound of the owl calling to you, plant your bare feet on the fertile earth, feel your shimmering creative essence brew inside your womb. Then look up at the sky.

The moon is shining on you, waiting for you to dance with her.
And under one wild moon, I will be there dancing with you.
May your creations be rooted in Earth and birthed with the moon.

 *Moon Ritual: Lunarized Water*

Your Sacred Items

-) A bowl (not plastic; glass or pottery); ideally it can be kept for sacred moon rituals
-) A favorite crystal you want to charge with moonlight
-) Herbs from your garden or a local source, such as mugwort, rose, nettle—or another drinkable herb you feel called to

Your Moon Ritual

-) Clean your bowl out with warm water and salt.
-) Imagine the bowl as symbolic of your inner pelvic bowl.
-) Now fill the bowl with fresh water, preferably from a well or spring but tap water will do.
-) Place your crystal in the middle of the bowl, representing the pelvic heart.
-) Sprinkle a pinch of magical herb in the bowl, invoking the spirit of the herb.
-) Place the bowl outside overnight on a full moon or a new moon.
-) Imagine the full moon is charging your pelvic bowl with lunar energy.
-) Imagine the new moon is gently cleansing and renewing your pelvic bowl.
-) In the morning take a sip of the lunar water as a sacrament.
-) Offer the rest of the lunarized water to the earth as a blessing.

SIX

MENSTRUAL MAGIC

Restoring Our Balance

Women reclaiming their lunar cycles and menstrual power is an act of revolution.

We are experiencing a lunar crisis in our world—we have become disharmonious with the rhythm of the moon and wisdom of our wombs. Our womb blood, which is coded with the secrets of life, is treated as if it were a curse, rather than a primordial feminine blessing.

Without the feminine rhythm of balance and the reverence of the blessed womb, our world is becoming dangerously unstable, as humankind continues to live in a way that is unsustainable.

Like the moon and lunar energy, Earth's resources, and our own inner resources, are also cyclical—they need time to rest and to renew. Earth also has a womb space, rich with red lava. Likewise, when this red river of molten fire erupts, it also creates and births new lands.

For thousands of years the moon and the feminine moon cycles of menstruation have been demonized, obscured, and hidden away with shame. We even find that some modern New Age theories continue this demonization, containing a subtle antifeminine agenda.

Ancient Moon Rays of Wisdom

The psychic spiritual power of the moon was once the origin of ancient religion: the lunar ray was revered as the source of creative, generative, and growing power that also held the power of darkness to dissolve, destroy, recreate, and rebirth. The moon was the original weaver.

In ancient China, the new moon—traditionally the time of menstruation—was officially proclaimed by heralds sent out by the royal astronomer. The community would plant crops and cast benevolent spells of sacred intentions under the mysterious light of the new-birth moon.

It was also common for earth-centered traditions to offer moon blood to the land and plants.

In the lands of Caanan, Astarte was worshipped in her guise as the Ashera, the sacred moon tree of knowledge and immortality—a deep symbol of feminine magic. Sabbaths to celebrate the new moon were held in sacred groves, until Yehovah banished the holy Moon Mother.

Earth Is Also a Lunar Being

Our entire world is undulating in a lunar wave, swaying and moving with her dark and light rhythms. Back in the fourth century BCE, Aristotle reported on the moon rhythms in all living creatures. A woman's ovaries swell at the time of the full moon, and this also happens for sea creatures, such as sea urchins. Oyster populations also fluctuate with the rhythms of the moon, which is why they are considered an aphrodisiac, infused as they are with feminine lunar magic.

Many plants also have lunar cycles, and gardening by the moon was one of the central feminine arts, to grow food that was in harmony with the cycles of life. Seeds swell with water during germination, and the maximum intake of water happens at the full moon and new moon, following the creative powers of the moon.

In 1971 it was discovered that honeybees also live in lunar consciousness. If the honeycomb has a north-south alignment, the hive is most active on the full moon. If their honeycomb has an east-west alignment, they fly out on new moon. The bees, always mythically sacred to the Goddess, follow a lunar rhythm.

Owls, who are considered to be a magical totem of the feminine, also follow lunar rhythms, from making mating calls on the full moon, to humming on the new moon, and ovulating and laying eggs in tune with the moon cycles.

Let the Menstrual Moon Magic Awaken

The moon's magnetic forces influence our psyche, our soul, our feminine being, often repressed in our unconscious, no matter what our gender is. The more untouched this aspect of our being is, the more extreme our reactions are to the moon's magic and menstrual blood.

The moon is calling to us with her gentle rays because we have forgotten the soft glow of her light and the dazzling, reflective brightness of feminine magic she brings to our psyche.

Lunar Magic: Reconnecting to Moon Cycles

☽ Gaze directly into the sky and receive the lunar ray on the full and new moons.

☽ Lunar trinity: Lunar magic works with the symbolic power of three (rebirth)
   1. New moon—a time to start new projects, make intentions, charge crystals, meet a new lover
   2. Full moon—a time to make commitments, celebrate life, do money magic, visit sacred sites
   3. Dark moon—a time to rest, let go, spend time alone or in reflection, do ancestral work

☽ If you menstruate, note the day your moon time starts and what astrological house the moon falls in on that day. Often we bleed with a specific energy of star wisdom.

World ✦ Tree

SEVEN

MOON MYSTIC
The Mysteries of Midnight

I am a child of the moon. Here where we live, every evening before bed, I go outside to visit the night. Sometimes the night is a soft velvet darkness that embraces me, other times it is mysterious and otherworldly, other times downright scary. I watch as the moon cycles, and the stars glitter in the vast blackness.

In more solar-based spiritual systems, rising with the sun to meditate is considered a virtue, yet I come alive when the moon rises and midnight approaches. My spiritual DNA lives deep in ancient moon colleges and feminine lunar mystery schools. In ancient witch traditions, it was believed that midnight was the ideal time to perform feminine magic or receive oracles and was an alchemical counterpoint to midday, when the sun rises into its highest solar transmission.

As a young girl, in my teens, I would often stay awake until midnight when the large grand(mother) clock in our house chimed twelve times. I would then get up to make spells and invocations using feminine mirror magic (which is believed to be most potent at midnight).

Often I wouldn't fall asleep until 3 a.m., another magical portal in feminine lore when it is believed the veils between the world are thinnest and souls enter and leave the earth realm.

It is interesting to note that nowadays we consider a good night's sleep to consist of eight hours sleeping straight through, ideally going to bed early and rising early.

Yet before the advent of modern lighting, our ancestors had different sleep patterns. People slept in smaller bursts, often napping in the day and reveling under the moon at night. The strict line between night and day didn't always apply. Nighttime, with its frequency of lunar feminine consciousness, was a time of magic.

Over the past one hundred years, our bodies and psyches have had to adapt to living under artificial light (in many ways!). Yet our instinctual self is still attuned to the past three million years of living under natural light and to the cycles of the sun and moon.

In his book on the history of dreaming, Robert Moss tells how even a few hundred years ago most people's internal rhythms meant they did not sleep all through the night. Instead, they often awoke in the night and entered a liminal space of active imagination and creativity, where new ideas and insights downloaded. Records of people's lives in these times refers to a second sleep, as it was known that people had two phases of sleep in the night, along with a magic doorway of consciousness.

Just as there are flowers that only bloom under moonlight, so there are parts of our deep feminine psyche that come alive at night under the mysteries of moonlight.

Resources

Moss, Robert. *The Secret History of Dreaming*. Novato, Calif.: New World Library, 2010.

EIGHT

FEMININE ALCHEMY

Embracing Transformation

These places of possibility within ourselves are dark because they are ancient and hidden; they have survived and grown strong through that darkness. Within these deep places, each one of us holds an incredible reserve of creativity and power, of unexamined and unrecorded emotion and feeling. The woman's place of power within each of us is neither white nor surface; it is dark, it is ancient, and it is deep.

AUDRE LORDE, FROM "POETRY IS NOT A LUXURY"

A tell-tale sign that a big transformation is brewing is that we leave linear time. We feel suddenly as if there is no connection to the past, as if it is a different country, but the future does not feel nearby or discernible either. It can be very disorienting. We often feel *magical terror.* A knowing change is coming. It's different from the "now," as a peak spiritual moment. It's more like sailing on a little boat in a big circular ocean of unknowing, with no horizon to navigate by.

We are being invited to "dwell in Possibility." This can be a mystical experience at times, but often it is like being slowly cooked in a transformational amniotic soup.

You are being served up as the main course of a recipe from a vast divine intelligence. This calls us into the feminine art of being—waiting and listening to life's whispers. If we try and push, force or do, our little boat turns in circles or, worse, capsizes. We imagine ferocious storms brewing on the unseen horizons or sharks circling us. Yet we also sense deep in our hearts that we will reach land and a new world awaits us that is full of promise and magical new potentials. The vital ingredient is trust. Reaching land is when time starts again, like a cosmic clock—and we get the chance to live our dreams, while weaving our past and future back together. This is the time for integration, grounding, and rooting. We birth back into the light again. Until that vast black ocean beckons us for our next "sailing trip"!

This oceanic realm is a feminine, mystical space pregnant with possibility. Just as a gestating baby needs to spend its time in the dark wonder of the womb to complete its destiny and be prepared for the new birth into the light of the world, you need to trust the waiting time. Often in this time of pregnant possibility, we are on the edge of a quantum leap. And in the riddling, paradoxical way of the feminine mysteries, we must learn to dance inside the Void.

 ### *The Feminine Dimension: How to Dwell in Mystery*

D Remove any time limits or linear markers from your journey. How would you move, feel, and live if there were no goal or agenda?

D Embrace paradox and the double-dragon-headed nature of truth: two opposing feelings or opinions can both be true at the same time.

D Sit still with your energy, make no plans, make no judgments, don't fix anything; when this gets uncomfortable then it truly becomes a spiritual practice.

D Learn to read the omens and the signs without grasping at a meaning.

D Notice things, pay attention, listen: What is the deep feeling inside you?

D Make space for your dreams and to journey into their symbols and feelings.

D Honor your deep knowing that it is time to rest in the lunar feminine mystery.

D Trust your intuition that you will know when it is time to birth into the light.

Resources

Lorde, Audre. *Sister Outsider: Essays and Speeches.* Revised edition. Berkeley: Crossing Press, 2007.

NINE

SPIRIT KEEPERS OF THE WOMB

Water Bearers, Fire Keepers

I t is time we allow the elemental beings to support and teach us.

Back in the winter of 2017, as the world started to spin on its axis a little wilder and weirder, both personally and collectively, I wrote down this wisdom from the spirit of the elements that I had received. It kept me nourished through difficult times, reminding me of our feminine magic.

Back then I wrote: Here in the Appalachian Mountains, where Azra and I live, spring is slowly, surely coming alive. In many ways, it's been a long, deep winter. Literally and figuratively.

It's been interesting to compare our luxurious, slow, silent descent into snow wisdom, with the outer frenzy and fury on the social media streams that also penetrate our lives.

We live on a mountain, above a river valley, and when it snows, we are often called into a shamanic internment within our home, unable to leave until the melt comes. Neither of us have smartphones, and I don't have a cell phone at all (I'm allergic). We don't have central heating either, and a log fire is our primary source of heat.

There is a famous Buddhist saying: "Enlightenment, then chop wood." For Azra, six months of the year, this is more than just a saying. Every morning, come rain, shine, or snow, he goes outside to chop wood for the fire that will keep us all warm that day. Often the cats are giving him beseeching eyes, and I am still snuggled in bed.

Somedays, in "remote" parts of the house (like the bathroom and near the windows), the temperature indoors has gone below freezing, while it's been minus 10 outdoors. Many of my beauty potions and products completely freeze over.

Wisdom of the Fire Keepers

Yet winter has so much to teach us, and I appreciate being able to sit and listen. Firstly, with no heat other than a fire, I begin to truly appreciate warmth—and I am viscerally brought into a circle with my ancestors, who understood the sacred power of fire. On cold nights out here, it can be the difference between life and death.

The elementality of winter also brings us—if we choose—into deep presence.

Although Azra starts the fire, often, throughout the day, I am the fire keeper—tasked with watching and tending the fire to make sure it doesn't fade and go out.

Even a fire that is burnt down to its final embers can miraculously resurrect, with a few strategic prods, but if it is allowed to truly die out, it is hard to bring back to life.

My fire tending at home is sometimes haphazard. If I am not really in my body or noticing my surroundings, when I finally look up from my fugue—the fire is out. So it has become an art for me, over the years, to be involved in something—writing, emails, online—yet still notice my body, and my outer world, and to stay tuned in.

It's interesting, because in the spiritual worlds, we often talk about flame keepers, and tending to a fire is a lesson on the lived reality of this. I can't help but reflect on this natural wisdom. What we tend to grows and blooms; what we forget, dies out.

What flame can we not afford to let go out?

What I've learned is that keeping the flame is a journey of slow steps, not big leaps. Every single day we are making deeply important choices. Seemingly small choices. Where do we put our focus? Who and what do we give attention to? What are we conceiving, gestating, nourishing, and preparing for a successful birth?

Because every distraction, every time our attention gets sucked in the wrong direction, often by strategies designed to do so, somewhere a fire is dying out.

Often the flame that is withering is within us. What keeps your flame strong?

 ## The Wisdom of Snow Maiden

Also, keep close to you the wisdom of snow. Recently, we spent time in the Diné (Navajo) lands and near the Hopi territories. I discovered Snow Maiden, a kachina that represents spirits, blessings, weather, and winter. In drought lands, such as Arizona, snow is more prized than rains. Snow drenches the land with moisture in a digestible way; it allows the earth to get deeply soaked. Sometimes a downpour will just run right off the hardened, sun-baked land. But snow gets down to the roots; it stays long enough to give back true nourishment. Snow Maiden is the beauty and magic of that cold, water-drenched wisdom.

Sometimes life snows on us—and it's bleak, cold, and seemingly endless. Let that snow seep in, because it might just be rich with something your inner landscape needs. One season's snow becomes the fertility that fuels our summer blossoming.

During our time out West, we visited a Diné medicine woman in her nineties who lives without running water or heat and whose home is a traditional hogan. We prepared by learning some basic Diné vocabulary and how to respectfully circle the hogan and greet the medicine woman. Speaking the Diné language, with a translator, she told us that Arizona was in a long drought period and laughed, saying we should bring her "some of that mountain rain."

As we left, the skies broiled over, gray clouds moved in, and rain started spitting down from the skies, before frosting over into a soft flutter of snowfall that began to blanket and feed the land. Later on, in our own red clay hogan, we watched awestruck as snow fell like fluttering angels through the central hole, open to the sky. It was as if our elemental prayers had been answered.

The elements are alive, and they listen to us, and if we are blessed, they answer back.

Life is moving pretty fast right now. Tune into the snow and fire.
What waters you and helps you digest more nourishment in your life?
What gets your fire rising and brings you warmth, energy, and excitement?

The path of feminine enchantment is all about the practical magic of being impeccable in our world so we can weave beauty and harmony.

 *Elemental Invocation*

Earth Ritual

Roots you and grows you: grounding, stillness, fertility
Invocation: "May I be rooted into Earth."
Feminine magic: cave, womb, lodge, rebirth

☽ Take a bowl of organic earth. Hold it in your hands; rub it into any places on your body you wish. Sit in silence for ten minutes; feel roots growing down your spine into Mother Earth.

Fire Ritual

Warms you and transforms you: releasing, activating, illumination
Invocation: "May I be lit up by my inner fire."
Feminine magic: dance, release ceremony, offering

☽ Put on a favorite dance track from when you were a teenager. Light a candle and spend ten minutes dancing your desire awake and tuning into your coming-of-age energy and passion.

Air Ritual

Expands you and lifts you: vision, inspiration, soul flight

Invocation: "May I fly high with my true vision."

Feminine magic: mountain, incense, spirit travel

☽ Light a stick of incense and sit carefully watching the smoke rise up into the sky. Allow a vision or prayer to rise from deep inside your body knowing and rise into the heavens on the smoke.

Water Ritual

Holds you and moves you: cleansing, soothing, surrender

Invocation: "May I be cleansed and renewed by water."

Feminine magic: baptism, chanting, renewal

☽ Pour water into a crystal cup. Blow across the surface of the water and run your finger along the rim three times clockwise to open the portal, sending prayers to the water. Then take a sip.

Magic Studies

Feminine Mystery Schools

One of the reasons why J. K. Rowling's Harry Potter series captured the imagination of the world, especially the magical school Hogwarts, is that we know in our bones we need a new vision of education for our world. Our souls are calling for cathedrals of learning and temples of the feminine arts, where we gather together to learn about inspired possibilities and to awaken our creative and magical powers, rather than being groomed for a life of financial servitude by a hyperlogical, mechanical system.

We are thirsting for modern-day magic schools, "yoniversities"—temples of the soul, whose core curriculum is the awakening of the human soul, which teaches practical, embodied feminine arts and sacred alchemical sciences. Our current academic systems were once rooted in astounding mystery schools and moon colleges, where initiates learned to be magical shamans of human possibility. Where men and women studied together and birthed new paradigms of genius. Some of the greatest alchemists and visionary scientists came from these traditions.

We are being called to pick up the wisdom thread again and rebirth temples of education and initiation for a modern world, to create our mystical schools of learning again—where ritual, intuition, sacred healing arts, and visionary science weave together. Where people can learn about the forbidden herstory of Earth.

This vision is just a choice away. The old system of cultural values is redundant, crumbling. It no longer has roots in the fertile imaginal field of living creativity. It is now time to focus on what we wish to build, how we wish our world to look. Children learn through reflection and mirroring. What world shall we show them?

Our world is calling for modern mystery schools and moon colleges, dedicated to birthing the new temples of learning where we can discover our genius and creative power. The wizards and witches of wisdom are awakening and birthing a new magical reality.

Well of Memory

Find the sacred well
By the lake of memory
Maidens protect the waters

Tell them:

> *I am a child of the mother*
> *And of the cosmic stars*
> *But my being is heavenly*

> *This you know:*
> *I am thirsting*
> *In this wasteland*

> *Give me cold water*
> *From the primordial memory*

They will give you water
Poured from the sacred spring

AUTHOR INTERPRETATION FROM THE
GREEK *HYMNS TO ORPHEUS*

Growing Our Roots

ELEVEN

MOTHER MOUNTAIN

Land of the Grail Goddess

Castleton village, underneath Mam Tor, and the surrounding villages of the Peak District in the north of England, has one of the last living Goddess worship traditions in England. Dating back at least three thousand years, magical Celtic rites of the Goddess are practiced, including well dressings and rites symbolic of sacred kingship and queenship.

The night is velvet dark like treacle, as if the black sky is pouring a magical substance into the world and rooting it back to the earth after dusk sets. The 350-million-year-old mountains surround us, silhouetted in the dark, like the mammoth spines of mythical dragons, resting in the flesh of the landscape. Magic is afoot.

Everything is so still. I can almost believe I slipped through a fissure in the dimension of existence and am back someplace so old time has not yet been invented.

I am returned to my ancestral homelands in the north of England, and an energy is uncoiling in the DNA of soil and bone and soul and home, reminding me how the winding path of our life is always rooted in its beginnings, where treasures lie.

The cool summer night is throbbing with energy and memories; the stars spelling out secrets like braille in the sky. On the hill a ruined castle stands, once given to the forbidden son of a long-ago king, and now slowly unwinding its sentry over the village of Castleton, passing it back to the spirit of the land and the ancestors.

Standing at the geological junction of the Dark Peak and White Peak, Winnats Pass, with its creviced gorge, dramatically descends into the Hope Valley, a sacred heart of the Peak District, with its rolling shires and heather-filled moors.

Tiny stone cottages cling to the edge of a wide stream flooding out from the belly of the hill. Locals call the stream *Styx*—the name for the mythological river that marks the boundary between Earth and the Underworld. The ruins of Peveril Castle perch high above on the crag, with a dramatic cave entrance gorged out below. Peak Cavern beckons, the Womb of the Earth Mother, distilling the deep darkness like a witch's brew. The sacred passageway into Peak Cavern is magnetic; it pulls you in. It is a terrestrial black hole. The magnetic darkness is so terrifying to the modern world, the cavern entrance is now called the Devil's Arse by both locals and guidebooks. Once it was the Devi's Vagina—the life-death-rebirthing passageway of the Goddess.

North England
Land of the Holy Grail

The north of England, often thought of as the wasteland of the Industrial Revolution, is also the homeland of the Holy Grail and the Goddess who keeps it. Stray outside the busy cities and suburbs, and you enter a land deeply imbued with ancient secrets.

The peak district is home to a number of mermaid legends, a secret nod to the ancient feminine priestess traditions—where "mermaids" who inhabited seas or lakes were the female shamans and faerie spirits who guarded the sacred waters of life, and who were known as Maidens of Mary. *Mer, mar, mari, mary,* and *mor* are all ancient feminine words for the sacred womb waters of the Great Mother, which held the mysteries of birth, death, and rebirth.

One of the best-known legends is that of the Mermaid's Pool, which lies under the western shoulder of Kinder Scout, the Peak District's highest point. It is said that a beautiful mermaid lives in a cave there and comes out to bathe in the pool every day. Local myths say that if you are lucky enough to see her on Easter Eve, you will be granted immortality—reflecting lost ancient traditions of resurrection and rebirth water rituals that were conducted by female "mermaid" priestesses during the sacred spring rites.

Lower down in the peak district is the prehistoric Arbor Low Stone Circle, described as the "Stonehenge of the Peak District"—a Neolithic ceremonial site surrounded by Bronze Age barrows and laced with powerful ley lines. At Gardom's Edge in Derbyshire, near Baslow, stones bearing distinctive cup and ring carvings mirror similar markings found in other northern sites and across the world. These petroglyphs carved onto natural boulders are the mysterious megalithic art of the Goddess—the cup, ring, spiral, and labyrinth all being symbols of the great Womb.

Some scholars say the Holy Grail legends were rooted in Northern England and only migrated farther down south as time went on. The Lady of the Rings was forgotten.

Mam Tor
Ancient Mother Mountain

It's the end of August holiday, and I'm lying on the grass on top of the grave of my father, held in the awesome presence of Mam Tor—an ancient dragon mother mountain, which was occupied thousands of years ago by those who followed the ways of the Goddess. My dad had a green burial, so only a tree marks his grave. The light is shimmering, a womb of ancient trees surrounds us. I can feel Dad's presence. He is at home here. This is the land of his—and my—ancestors.

What are *the ancestors*? I've been percolating on this since my father died and was buried in the foothills of Mam Tor back in 2013. There is an ancestral soul of our lineage and an ancestral soul of the land. It is like a genetic grail that holds parts of us together and weaves with the missing parts of those who went before. Our entire lineage is a vast web being spun across time from these parts.

Our healing comes from stitching these time lines back into wholeness. We do not leave anyone behind. Our ancestral web spans back to the start of time and laces forward into the very end of time. Our stories, our past, needs to be rethreaded.

Where once the world had a goddess and a queen, she was dethroned, her memory lost, her garland dropped. The weathered hills are calling us to remember again.

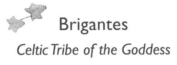 Brigantes

Celtic Tribe of the Goddess

On top of Mam Tor are burial chambers thousands of years old, and family burials in Treak Cliff Cavern at the base of the mountain suggest that Neolithic people lived around Castleton 7,500 years ago. Mam Tor was also home to Celtic tribes who lived in terraced round houses on the peak almost three thousand years ago. This indigenous Celtic tribe called the Brigantes worshipped a goddess called Brigantia, who some believe is related to the goddess Brighid, and her memory lives on in the land. In the 1970s an ancient stone head sculpture of their goddess was found in a garden in the village of Castleton, at Rose Cottage, site of the village's ancient well, and where the Garland Ceremony started every year in May. The sculpture is three thousand years old.

The Brigantes were led by a powerful queen, and their goddess Brigantia was adopted by the incoming Romans almost two thousand years ago, who also associated her with their goddess Minerva. Sites of Celtic tribes who worshipped Brigantia are found across France too, though the Pennines—the dragon spine of mountains across north Britain—were especially sacred sites. It is possible that even the name for Britain originates from the goddess Brigantia. The word *brigantes* means "high or noble ones" and also "highlanders." It is an honorific name for the Bright Ones of legend and myth. Brigantia's name means "the High Goddess." In Irthington in Yorkshire, an ancient inscription calls her "divine nymph Brigantia"—and there were many healing shrines dedicated to her magical powers. Brigantia was a Womb goddess of rebirth, associated with spring rites, with wells, streams, rivers, and water cults. Sacred rituals, such as well dressings and Castleton's Garland Ceremony, have likely descended down to us, in an unbroken line, from these ancestors and their goddess.

I can feel the ancestors around me, whispering in the wind, reminding me. Their dimension is just a hair's breadth away from us, and in the right light, when the air stills, I can almost see their old Neolithic village and hear their songs on the wind.

Yorkshire's Secret Church of the Goddess

Yorkshire, with its wild moors and peaks, wore its conversion to Christianity lightly, carrying on its ancient pagan goddess-worshipping rituals and ceremonies, as usual, right up to the modern day, with iPhones capturing the May Queen in all her glory.

The new religion was neatly tucked, like a suckling babe, into the Womb of the Great Mother rites, a religious tradition dating back at least three thousand years (which artifacts show) and no doubt stretching back hundreds and thousands of years before that. The memories of those rituals are etched into the stones and moss.

I was baptized in my local Yorkshire church, and later on in my childhood, I went to another local village church hall where I attended weekly Brownie meetings, as a Girl Guide. We danced around a big replica of a red and white toadstool, like the faerie folk of old, holding hands and weaving with the left path. We called our leader Brown Owl. I remember the vivid red of the toadstool blurring into a red circle of light, as we danced faster and faster round the circle. I was eight years old, and it was exhilarating. The red and white toadstool is symbolic of the left-hand path of the fay and the feminine pathways and is the *Amanita muscaria* used in the witch's brew for shamanic initiations to alter consciousness so initiates could "fly" to the Otherworld.

When the spring buds were vivid green and the cherry tree in our garden bloomed pink and the hawthorn bush bloomed white, it was Maytime. At the back of the church hall, we would dance the Maypole, dressed in white, decked with flowers, holding tight to the ruby red silk ribbon our hands would weave with. We would visit the larger villages in the Peak District for the well dressings and May celebrations. I remember seeing the May Queen adorned and enthroned, being driven round the village on a float, followed by a brass band and the rest of the folk.

My auntie was very religious: she was a devoted part of the church community in her village, helping organize the well dressings and all the yearly festivals. She was a brilliant flower arranger, and when we went to visit, she was often crafting or engaged in some feminine art or other. I sense her religious devotion also included the well of feminine wisdom, decked with flowers, and scented with the first dew of spring. My soul was held in these celebrations, as if an ancient essence was pouring into me, tincturing me with deep memory, infusing me with the lost feminine rites.

Well Dressing
The Flowering Vulva of the Well

From time out of mind, the Goddess and her regenerative powers have been associated with water and celebrated and honored at Earth's fountains of life—streams, springs, rivers, and wells. Symbolically, the spring and the well represent the magical vulva of the Goddess, streaming forth the blessed waters of healing.

Well dressings are a continued living tradition of Goddess and Womb worship still practiced in the Peak District, Derbyshire, but now subsumed into the church, in a marriage of convenience of old custom and new religion. In the village of Tideswell, records show that well dressings have been going

Well dressing, Welsh Borders, United Kingdom

for at least 750 years but likely continue on from the Celtic traditions of the goddess Brigantia and her holy waters.

In a beautiful sacred feminine art, living artwork is created out of wildflowers and natural fauna, such as a leaves and acorns, and used to decorate the well. Now the pictures often feature Christian subjects, but in old custom, the mouth of the well would have been decorated with flowers and sacred offerings to honor the feminine.

In the Peak District, well dressings are usually celebrated conjunct to a festival called Wakes, which starts the Saturday nearest to the Saint's Day of John the Baptist. This feast day was superimposed upon the prior midsummer celebrations, closely timed with the summer solstice.

On St. John's Eve, wise women would go to collect herbs or practice vulvic magic in the fields.

The Wakes Week is a weeklong revelry of festivals and celebrations that starts with a traditional torchlight procession, accompanied by music and Morris dancing. This festival, which is still celebrated to this day by the local community, is an incredible window into the grail rites of the Goddess and the true meaning of queenship.

During the week's festivities, Wakes royalty are crowned: a young girl becomes the Wakes Queen, and a younger girl becomes the Rosebud Princess. The duties of the newly crowned "royalty" include serving as ambassadors for the village for the coming year. Royalty was a role of community service, not an elite privilege.

Garland Ceremony
The King and His Consort

Castleton continues the flower-strewn path of the Goddess with its annual Garland Ceremony, which usually takes place on May 29 every year, also coinciding with Oak Apple Day.

Part of the ancient fertility and cosmic regeneration mysteries, the ceremony celebrates the rebirth of spring, delivered from the dark womb of winter and the dark face of the Goddess. Likely, this Maytime ceremony is a long-lost daughter of the ancient Celtic rituals where ancestors would have participated in a living mystery play with the land.

At the heart of this sacred ceremony is a garland created from local wild foliage, with vividly colored flowers and greenery woven onto a beehive-shaped frame. The garland is worn by the ceremonial king and fits over his head and shoulders, shrouding him within the mystery of the feminine womb, the beehive of the queen.

The topmost piece of the garland is called the queen, and this most sacred piece of the adornment is removable and can be separated from the main frame. It literally "crowns" the king when he ritually places this part over

The king wearing a crown of flower garlands, Garland Day, Castleton, Peak District

The king riding with his consort

his head. It is beautifully suggestive of the masculine returning to the interior Womb of the Great Mother to receive his initiation into the feminine and to be anointed king. As he enters deep inside the flower of her creation, within the birthing place of the mystery, we can almost imagine the sacred sexual rites this symbolizes. It also reflects the Celtic tradition of the sovereignty goddess, where only the spirit of the land, believed to be feminine, could crown a king and grant him the right to rule.

After his "crowning," the king, wearing the garland of the spirit of the land, rides on top of a horse in procession with his consort—a woman from the local community.

Preparation for this ancient goddess ceremony begins the night before, when oak and other greenery is fixed to all but one of the pinnacles on the church tower, and wild, sweet-scented flowers are gathered to decorate the garland—such as voluptuous pink peonies, purple-tinted wallflowers, and white lily of the valley.

In past times, the Garland Dressing took place at Rose Cottage, overlooking the rushing stream coming from deep with the womb caves of the nearby Tor—and where a sacred well, which once replenished the entire village with water, lives. The base of the garland is traditionally decorated by the men, while the flowery queen, which crowns the king, is decorated only by women of the community.

During the procession, young village girls dressed in white and adorned with posies of flowers dance the Maypole circle at each stop on the procession way. They carry a garland stick, which resembles a miniature Maypole, with red, white, and blue ribbons, the traditional colors of witchcraft, representing the birth-death-rebirth moon mysteries of the Goddess.

Young women from the community dance around the Maypole on Garland Day.

Women adorned with posies of flowers or green leaves or flower crowns

The procession weaves its way to the village church, but because of the obvious old pagan origins of the ceremony, the queen is not allowed inside the church. Instead, the exiled flowery queen crown is removed and hoisted onto the church tower, where she remains until her flowers wilt.

The Cosmic Eucharist of the Sacred Feminine

These sleepy villages have been quietly upholding the ancient goddess traditions of their ancestors, honoring the land in her cyclical seasons of life-death-rebirth. Often unknowingly, they have carried the legacy of the Grail, which renews the land and heals the people by intimate relationship with a living sacred feminine landscape.

What these living traditions still bring to the human psyche is of immeasurable value. As a collective consciousness, we are thirsting for the feminine waters, which birthed all humanity—this is our true soul heritage and the forgotten heritage of the soul of the land. I know these rituals rang true and clear in my own inner world, resonating with a deep archetype, bringing a vision of how we may heal and renew.

Often these ancient ceremonies are dismissed as "empty pagan ritual"—as if there is not a living, spiritual tradition of transformational awakening that lies within them. Yet the Goddess rites live at the heart of the mystical Christian traditions too, which also hold this transformational power of renewal, if we remember the sacred queen who crowns, anoints, and heals and allow her back into the church again.

I pondered this incredible living tradition, still being enacted here in my homeland. I lay on my father's grave, held within an ancient landscape of immeasurable origins, where the wisdom of our ancestors waits for us to ask again: Whom does the Grail serve? Closing my eyes, breathing deeply, sinking into Earth's arms, I ask . . .

On the whispers of the wind, my dad replies—a voice threaded in ancestral wisdom. He tells me of a grand cosmic eucharist we all belong to. How everything is digested and eaten and transformed and rebirthed inside the Womb of the Great Mother. How we become at one with everything in a mystical feasting of union with God. Nothing is left out, or left behind, nothing dies, nothing is separate. It is all included and embraced.

Resources

Castleton Garland Committee.

Castleton Historical Society (castletonhistorical.co.uk).

Edwards, Eric. "Brigantia, Goddess of the Brigantes," December 3, 2015. Eric Edwards Collected Works (website).

McGrath, Sheena. *Brigantia: Goddess of the North*. N.p.: Lulu Books, 2015.

Smith, Roly. *Myths and Legends of the Peak*. Ashbourne, UK: Ashbourne Editions, 2012.

TWELVE

DOMESTIC WITCHERY

Creating Your Nest

We live in a culture that often celebrates leaving the nest or flying the nest.

In symbolic terms these are the initiatory gateways—where we leave the familiar, comforting boundaries of our being to forge a transformational path.

Stories abound of gurus or saints, often male, who leave the warm hearth of the family home to wander free, teaching that we need nothing in this life.

But the wise ways of the Womb know that just as we must oftentimes depart old shores and migrate to new states of consciousness, we must also remember to come home to roost, to nest and integrate and enjoy the fruits of our journeys.

Sometimes it takes greater courage to stay in the cauldron of life than to leave.

The energy of going outward, taking bold leaps, embracing change, and truth, reaching for freedom is a beautiful masculine flow of movement in our lives.

But so often we forget, overlook, or diminish the more feminine qualities of coming home, building, nesting, patience, tending to our home fires.

In this soft, grounded, cyclical energy our creations can grow and thrive.

The temple of our own homes can hold our deepest transformations: we

are returning home to the feminine, to our own center, to our womb space.

The energy of the home and the womb are intimately interwoven, and our relationship to home often reveals surprising insights into our womb.

Our power to build, manifest, thrive, and experience beauty and abundance in our lives depends on our rootedness in our center, in our womb—our home nest.

 ## The Power of Nesting

After our wedding at the magical Cae Mabon in Wales, I sat at the large oak table in the Hobbit-like dining room, browsing through a book by theologist Matthew Fox that lived on a creaky old bookshelf. I randomly flipped open a page, with the magnetic pull of a "Womb wink," a divine sign tap-dancing for my attention.

I alighted on this quote: "Trust can begin with the simple act of examining a bird's nest, for when we examine a nest, we place ourselves at the origin of confidence in the world, we receive a beginning of confidence, an urge toward cosmic confidence. Would a bird build its nest if it did not have its instinct for confidence in the world? A nest is a sign of optimism."

A warmth began to spread from within, as if the roots of Earth were calling to me with welcoming arms, saying, "Trust me daughter, it's safe, relax, let go, nest."

As a teenager I had donated my wedding fund to pay off my parents' mortgage, telling them I would never, ever get married. They might as well have the money (after it had been made clear I wouldn't be able to divert it to a traveling fund).

I dreamed of adventure, travel, doing things. I drank in stories of female artists, writers, poets, revolutionaries, spiritual visionaries who had dared to dream and to live out that dream and to leave behind the dull drudgery of the household.

Over time, I found a spiritual outlet for these masculine urges—the path of mystical yogis and mad saints who head out into the wilderness of the soul. Written between the lines of these spiritual adventure stories was a sniffing at the humdrum lives of the common householder who did unspiritual things, like birth, build, and love.

Growing up in a working-class world, where women spent their days polishing the chains that bound them to the kitchen sink, I had the same dismissive sniff. It felt like women who tended the nest were crushed, tired, uninspired, imprisoned—cleaning, cooking, doing menial jobs and full of unspoken, unfulfilled dreams.

I did not see the feminine soul initiations behind the tired eyes, the courage and strength it took to stay, the power of softness it took to hold the flame of love.

But soon enough, life offered out an invitation, a homecoming—to weave a new web, to revision the feminine realms, to revisit the imaginal cells of nesting.

The nest is our home, our container, our cauldron. Our crucible.

Home Is Where the Wildness Lives

In my search for a new way of being on Earth, I realized that patriarchy was not just peddling one false myth, but many—threaded through many paths.

But there was another way, a wild way, a truly feminine way—a Womb way, which lay forgotten but was singing to be remembered and embodied again. Simple, wild, with cycles arcing up among the skies and buried deep in the land.

A path that could stand still long enough to birth, that could journey with a sense of humor and a knowing wink, that could embrace seasons of grief and letting go and seasons of harvest, pleasure, bounty, and fertility and hold the thread of both.

A place brimming full with the soft pleasures and sweet ecstasies of life herself.

To be grounded, rooted, deep, still, now. We cannot feel it when we are running—physically, emotionally, energetically, or psychically. We have to come home.

We have to nest. Not to always be somewhere else.

Wild creatures know how to nest. They know how to leave—and how to return.

There is great spiritual power in pottering—in the garden, in the kitchen, just being around the house, the home. Tending the herbs in the garden, making a fresh-brewed tea, the sensual art of cooking. Or entering the prayer chamber of the sofa, lounging with God, in intimate conversations and occasional snoring.

Nowhere to go, nothing to do. No grand theories to unite. Just to relax and be.

Home brings us back down to Earth. It makes us real. It grants us "enrealment."

It is imbued with Womb magic; the power of Earth, of life, of love, of the real.

 ## Making a Womb Nest

I wildcrafted a nest for our altar, to tune in deeper with this great knowing of the natural world—that to nest is to show faith in creation and the web of life.

Pottering round the garden, I gathered my materials, collecting dry grass from the dying year that had just enough snow to soften it. All around me I could feel life stirring in the trees, and the birds were busy crafting their nests too.

I felt camaraderie with the birds; I felt them watching me with kind eyes. Singing loudly with glee as another season prepared to bloom and bear fruit.

Weaving the nest together was more difficult than I imagined—the dry grass was unruly, unyielding. I tried, and failed, a number of times, getting more annoyed.

Deep breaths, ground, I told myself. Then I looked to the skies and asked the birds for help—for their advice. They were the experts.

The answer came on the wind, soft with the breath of life.

Surrender, trust, patience. *Patience.* Keep weaving, however hard it feels. Even when things fall apart and seem impossible, keep weaving—keep trusting.

How quickly we give up in our fast, instant world, I realized.

So I began again, with softness, patience, finding a rhythm. Breathing. Trusting.

Magically, a nest began to form—a Womb circle of twigs, feathers, leaves.

I felt as if I were holding the soul of the world in my hands, so precious, nested with a million dreams and wishes and creations ready to be birthed.

I understood the power in building a home with our own hands, crafting our nest with love—like the birds. Now we buy our houses, rather than make our homes.

But the more we can touch, inspirit, weave, create, twig by twig, feather by feather, stitch by precious stitch, with the silk of our dream hearts— the more love and life is imbued into our creations and our world. This is Womb lore.

What do you wish to weave, to build, to touch, to create?

Life supports you and will magically provide all the materials you need.

A nest is also a chalice.

A holy grail.

Resources

Fox, Matthew. *Creativity: Where the Divine and Human Meet.* New York: TarcherPerigee, 2004.

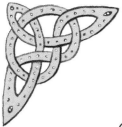

THIRTEEN

ROOTED POWER

Feminine Spiritual Path

There is a great feminine spiritual power in rooting that is often over-looked, ignored, or demoted in modern life and more masculine-based spiritual traditions.

It is true that life is impermanence and that the only constant is change.

Yet this continually flowing movement of life can also have roots, as well as wings.

Learning how to ground, root, commit, be still, and invest is part of the Goddess's wisdom ways and often the missing essence that will bring us into embodiment.

Being rooted is the key to manifestation, blooming, and intimate relation-ships. When we are uprooted and disassociated, our spirit cannot take seed and grow.

When we tune into some of the wisest beings on our planet, such as the sacred trees, we can see this natural feminine wisdom in action, and we can begin to feel experientially the qualities of rooted consciousness and the vast power it holds.

There is a divine patience and commitment to the everyday world that can heal it from within, yet so often we take fright and fly away from our life circumstances. We forget the power of gestation, trusting that something is unfolding in the dark.

Because much of religious and spiritual thought is based on patriarchal concepts, we often find ideas flying around that take us out of our bodies and the fertile muddy soil of relationship, bringing us new spiritual dogma that goes against natural wisdom.

Often these ideas plug into our traumatized psyche, which has had to flee the body and find safety at higher ground and is afraid to come back down and trust again. Of course, it is essential we stay connected to our true infinite source and keep ourselves reminded of the spirit that is untouched by our earthly travails—yet our spirit is desiring to come and nest fully in our physical form and in our lives.

By following the inner voice of our grounded feminine wisdom, we will be able to bloom the garden of our Earth, our families, our relationships, and our lives again.

Here are some of the spiritual ideas that often take us away from our deeper feminine knowing, our nous and common sense—bringing us up into the mind with its notions of what is "good" and "right" rather than flowing with what feels best.

Myth 1.
Needs Are Wrong, Lower, or Unspiritual

Nature's Wisdom: Everything in nature has needs, and if these needs are not met then the blueprint of creation cannot bloom to its fullest. Seeds need water, plants need sunlight, the soil needs to be fertile and rich with mineral supplies. Plants and animals also need each other and thrive best in a collaborative web consciousness.

Common Sense: Rather than deny our needs, we can examine deeply how and why our foundational needs are not being met either through our relationships, our environment, or our work. The journey is to water the garden of our life with love in ways that grow our potential, inner wealth, and happiness. This allows us to root into the miraculous potentials of our biology—rather than live in disassociated out-of-body states.

Our needs are part of our human creative blueprint, and we can celebrate them and take practical actions to birth what we need into our lives. By allowing ourselves to admit our needs, we open the doorway to true manifestation.

Myth 2.
We Should Always Be Unconditionally Loving

Nature's Wisdom: Accepting everything without conditions is not how nature thrives. Boundaries, limits, and conditions are an essential part of the creative process, and Earth often has natural processes to contain and prune its resources. Growth without limits often unsettles the natural balance and harmony of life. For example, cancer is a disease where cells keep multiplying without conditions or limits.

Common Sense: It is true that there is a universal love that permeates all of creation, yet in the embodied manifestation of life on Earth, conditions are actually included within this love. We may call it the laws of nature or Ma'at—the divine harmonic principles of the Mother Goddess. If we don't live by these conditions or laws of love, we will lose harmony with the web of life and each other. In kabbalah, it is known as the balance of Guverah and Chesed—also known as judgment and mercy. Chesed is the infinite outpouring of love, and Guverah is the restricting force that keeps everything in balance—making sure we don't give too much or spend our energy in inappropriate ways and that we are able to set healthy boundaries.

Myth 3.
There Is Nothing Broken—Everything Is Perfect

Nature's Wisdom: Earth is paradoxically very strong yet also very fragile. Although Earth has a powerful regenerative capacity, there is a natural ecosystem of interconnection and balance that if broken has harmful and unexpected consequences. We are living in modern times where we are waking up to the realization of how our disconnection from deep earth knowing is destroying the Earth Mother who supports us and causing pain, disease, and disharmony.

Common Sense: Matter may be infinite and indestructible at its spiritual root, yet that does not make it wise to take its finite expressions for granted and to ignore the tangible harm and hurt that can be caused to living life-forms—including ourselves. Anyone seeing a child in the aftermath of abuse knows that something has been broken—trust in life and a sense of safety on Earth. There is truth in knowing we never lose our innocence or place in the thread of love, and we do not need to be fixed from a perceived flaw of sin, lack, or imperfection. Yet we can feel broken and wounded by life through events that do not seem perfect, and by embracing this, grieving it, and allowing it to not be OK, deep healing can happen. Grief is feminine magic.

When we ground into the true reality of life—not the culture we inherited from our parents or disassociated cultural or spiritual theory and dogma but the majestic natural laws and principles of creation, our spiritual journeys are filled with creative power. Rather than being disempowered, stuck in flights of fancy that keep us circling in illusions, we begin to land into our own lives, with the power to birth new realities.

From this rooted place, we can start to birth the fruits of regeneration, redemption, and resurrection that all the ancient myths speak of. This is the heart of the feminine mysteries, the grail of our embodied consciousness, which restores the wasteland.

 *Your Sacred Balance*

Rooted Power

☽   Check inside your own body to feel what your deep needs are at this time.

☽   Check inside your own body to feel what boundaries you need to honor.

☽   Check inside your own body to feel what grief is living inside your heart.

Infinite Love

☽   Affirm that you deserve love and belong to the weave of Mother Earth's love.

☽   Affirm that there is an abundance of resources for you and other people.

☽   Affirm that your heart is a chalice full of the infinite presence of love.

FOURTEEN

ENDARKENMENT

God Is in the Soil

The soil is the unified realm we are all rooted into.

One day I was pondering on the idea of God—the ineffable being or energy so many people look to in the world for love, security, and support and that for many people takes the form of a man or a masculine father figure of infinite knowing and capacity to protect and love.

Likewise, other people prefer to embrace a divine mother or a goddess or feminine presence.

I could sense that we were imagining this great mysterious being or presence in our own image, as a mother and father, or a god or goddess. This could be a beautiful support system, but I wanted to go further or deeper. I wanted to enter that magical realm beyond humanness. So I went to have a chat with the wisest being I knew and ask the most mystical of questions.

Who, or what, is "God"?

I padded barefoot into the garden for this important, oracular consultation—my feet squelching into vivid green moss freshly scented from a summer rain. There she was, my go-to mentor.

With my hands placed on the gnarly old skin of her bark and my head sheltered by a cathedral of her green leaves forming a canopy above me, I asked the old maple tree what she knew.

She and I had a bond of trust, as every month I gift her my moon blood.

Slowly, as if drawing wisdom up from her deep roots like sap, she paused to consider.

Then she replied gently and decisively: "God is in the soil."

I must confess at first I was a little taken aback. I could feel that hidden in some subconscious part of me I'd been looking up to the sky for answers, not deep down into the darkness of dirt.

After I'd sat with it for a while it made sense, and it filled me with a quiet relief. *It made sense.* There was a *divine biome* that all of the creation was rooted into, an embodied womb of fertility.

When we are uprooted from the divine soil that grows us, we forget this unified source we all belong to and perceive ourselves as separated and different.

Plants have different forms in visible light, but their roots all stretch down into this unified source, the rich, fertile soil of Mother Earth, which they grew from and which feeds them.

In the same way we are all rooted into the unified field of energy that we can call the quantum field, dark matter, black light, void, emptiness, source, pleroma, or just plain old love.

We all look different and appear other in visible light, but at the root source of the divine darkness we unite. We must keep this soil fertile and root deep into it—we wither otherwise.

When we come together in love, or unite as lovers, in this union we return to this unified root. We experience the union of different forms in visible light, and the formlessness they grow from.

Humanity must remember this shared soil that we all grow from.

FIFTEEN

GRANDMOTHER WISDOM

Our Primordial Knowing

After my spiritual descent to the Womb of Earth in 2012 to commune with the soul of Earth, I was given a vision of the modern landscape of the current world. In the vision a very wise and seasoned grandmother sat on a porch, stitching and weaving, watching and listening, as the world went by. Suddenly, disrupting this beautiful, harmonious, and deep peace that settled around her, a young man sped into the neighborhood, riding a big, shiny motorbike at high speed, making lots of noise, drawing attention to himself, with the noisy exhaust pipe filling the sky with fumes. He raced through as if to say, "Hey, look at my power. Follow me. I know the way."

Grandmother sat watching, stitching, and raised a humorous eyebrow at this spectacle and gave a knowing smile as this very teenage, immature masculine energy passed through, full of bluster and bravado, thinking he was all-knowing. Seeing this energy, which is the essence of arrogance and every broken expression of false ego-driven power, through Grandmother's eyes, it appeared silly and downright ridiculous. It wasn't scary; it was comical in its desire to be noticed. Gradually, this disturbing energy passed through, and the peaceful stillness returned. Grandmother got back to her stitching and weaving, still chuckling deeply to herself.

This vision has stayed with me and unfolded. I became aware of how much of our world, including much of the world's spiritual teachings and cultural messages, come from this "prophet on a motorbike" energy—immature, masculine, know-it-all, pompous, full-of-itself energy. Its energy signature is extremist, loud, brash, attention-seeking, going too fast, making too much noise, disturbing others, pushing too hard. Yet it also offers distraction and "absolute certainty" to those who feel lost or confused.

This energy, which takes us out of harmony with life's cycles, is not about gender. We all have this immature, disconnected energy within us because it is the stuff the patriarchy is made of—glittering and strong, promising power and energy, yet ultimately destructive and at odds with the slow, organic, feminine energy of Earth.

I felt so deeply how much we now need the medicine of Grandmother Growth—the wise feminine elder, who intuitively knows how to grow life, understands the delicate balance that must be sought, both within ourselves and our inner world and also in the outer world, to live harmoniously within the vast web of life.

This wise crone energy can be spectacularly embodied in a flesh-and-bone woman who is coming into her mature ripeness and has truly done her work. But it can also be embodied within our own psyche, whether we are man or woman, no matter what our age. It is the wise inner voice that says: "Wait, have patience, don't push . . . trust." It is also the instinctive nous that calls us into true rooted action.

From this place a beautiful, soulful yang energy arises to help grow the garden, and the two flows of receptivity and activity come together in a creative lovemaking.

Ultimately, Grandmother Growth knows how to weave with the deep alchemy of true growth. She has midwifed many cycles and seen their demise. She keeps the primordial templates tucked under her flowerpots in the Eden realm she tends. She rests in a profound silence and stillness, which is the seed-space of all creation.

Ancient Grand Mother of Creation

I move in every creature . . .

I am the Invisible One within the All . . .

It is I who poured forth the water.

It is I who am hidden within radiant waters.

I am the one who gradually put forth the All by my Thought.

It is I who am laden with the Voice.

It is through me that Gnosis comes forth.

FROM *TRIMORPHIC PROTENNOIA,*

TRANSLATED BY JOHN D. TURNER (GNOSIS.ORG)

SIXTEEN

CRONE BLESSINGS

Celebrating Our Elders

Celebrating the sacred power and beauty of the crone,

Calling forth the rooted presence of the wise woman, the elder.

Her wisdom is forged so deep it is etched in prayer lines on her face.

Her body is a constellation of sacred songlines,

Each reaching down into a hidden storytelling.

Her memories shape themselves into a chalice of truth.

Her sexual life force is distilled into pure essence.

Her smile is graced with compassion that has drunk a lifetime of tears.

Her creative spirit is wild with mistakes and forgiveness.

Her wise blood flows deep within Otherworld,

Bringing rivers of knowing back to heal our world.

How can we live without her Wisdom Maps?

The sacred crone is the beginning and the end.

Her cauldron filled with rebirthing stars.

Her beauty is not of this world,

As she blesses us with wisdom.

SEVENTEEN

CELTIC MAGIC

Path of the Swan Priestess

In 2009 I began writing a novel on Mary Magdalene after visiting her pilgrimage site in St. Baume. Shortly afterward, I began to experience mysterious coincidences connected to the archetype and Celtic lineage of the swan, which I had no prior knowledge of.

Although it hadn't been included in my outline of the book, a new storyline emerged and wove itself into the book about the Pre-Raphaelite muses and a sisterhood of the swan, a lineage of long-lost swan priestesses, connected to the sacred feminine mysteries of the Goddess.

Later, sitting in womb meditation one day, I was jolted to feel the words *cygnus, cygnus, cygnus* vibrate repetitively into my womb, with a compelling urgency. I immediately got up and went to the internet to look it up. I had a vague idea the word *cygnus* had something to do with swans. Other than usual references to the swan, an article by Andrew Collins, author of *The Cygnus Mystery,* caught my eye.

I ordered his book, and when I received it and read it, a few key ideas struck me. One was the Cygnus black hole and the spiritual powers and potentials of black holes as cosmic wombs of creation. I felt that my womb had been pointing me to this key magical insight. The other piece of information that buzzed for me was the description of a swan cult in Northern Europe and an archeological site in Cornwall called Saveock, which had evidence of swan worship.

I tried to find out how to visit Saveock, but as a private archaeological site, it was not easy to find or visit, unlike Avebury or a stone circle. So I gave up for the moment.

During my shamanic journeying at this time, I received my womb name as Seren Swannesha. *Seren* is the Welsh word for "star," and *swannesha* is an Old English name meaning "gentle swan." It was also the name of a Saxon female mystic, Edith Swannesha or Edith the Fair, who had visions of the Virgin Mary and set up a shrine to Our Lady in Norfolk. During these shamanic journeys through my womb, I found I could "ride the swan" into the center of the universe—a black hole—for initiations.

In 2012, Azra and I were driving into Cornwall where we were to live for three months, after visiting the sacred site of Avebury, also a swan site. I mentioned how much I wanted to find and visit Saveock—this secret swan site that had proved so elusive to me. Shortly afterward, we visited a person who lived near St. Michael's Mount, who had been recommended as a musical instrument maker. In casual conversation, I mentioned my desire to find the Saveock site. Moments later, our new friend picked up the phone and dialed his sister-in-law—an experimental archaeologist who was custodian of the site and lived in a cottage on the land. It turned out that the dig was closing for the summer that weekend, and she invited us to come and visit.

Stunned by the coincidence, we drove up that weekend. As we entered the turnoff to access the land, "Song of the Siren" began to play on our stereo, even though we had not selected that song or pressed play. There was an aura of magic and mystery to this land that is unsurpassed in any place I have visited before or since.

The archaeologist gave us a guided tour of the site, showing us the "womb" pits that had been dug into the earth and the channel of water that had been diverted from the river to create a ritual bathing site, for purposes we can only intuitively know. The river was still known by local healers for the healing properties of its water.

Months later, we were invited to spend winter solstice 2012 at Saveock. And so, on a foggy and mysterious night, which the ancients had predicted was the opening of a birth portal for humanity seeding a new era, Azra and I found ourselves in a private ceremony in a small Celtic roundhouse on the site, just the two of us playing our newly crafted womb lyre and tuning into the memories of the ancient lands—and feeling the time lines merge and unify between past, present, and future. We could feel the flutter of swan magic, like angel wings, around us.

In 2014, we visited our lyre maker and discovered a beautiful but unfinished carved lyre in the shape of a swan. A man from India had originally commissioned it with the words that he wished to bring the "sound of heaven to earth," but he had since disappeared off the scene, leaving the swan lyre languishing without a home. We immediately claimed her! By another coincidence, in the novel I had been writing, there was a swan ball scene, with a harpist playing a swan-shaped instrument. I had no idea at that point that priestesses used to play swan-shaped lyres.

In 2015 the finished swan lyre was delivered to us in person by the lyre maker's wife, who traveled from England to Paris to make the delivery. Due to traffic problems, we could not get to the arranged meeting place and instead had to pull off into a random side road, park on the pavement, and then walk. Intuitively, I looked up at the street name as we set off—it was Rue de Cygne, Road of the Swan. After picking the swan lyre up, we headed straight to our next destination—Chartres. It was a symbolic moment typing "Rue du Cygne to Chartres" into the GPS system!

Finally, we delivered the manuscript for our book *Womb Awakening* on November 11, the date of the old swan feasts, and a priestess of Glastonbury sent us a swan painting.

The swan, symbol of the Great Mother, and her sacred lineages had guided us in many ways, weaving us along her path, a starlit way back to love and to the Womb.

Swan Cloak

Cape of the Shamaness

In Irish tradition, the bards would wear a cloak made of swan feathers to incant their poetry. This special shamanic cloak called a *tuigen* is associated with shamanic flight into the Otherworld.

In Irish mythology, Caer Ibormeith, a prince's daughter, would shape-shift into a swan every alternate Samhain, residing in her swan form for an entire year until the next Samhain. Mac Ind Olc, son of the Dagda and one of the Tuatha de Danann, searches for Caer Ibormeith in his dreams—where he finds her and 150 other women chained up in pairs at the lake of the Dragon's Mouth. Mac is told that if he can identify Caer Ibormeith in her swan form, he can marry her. He chooses correctly, and they both fly to the River Boyne as swans. During their swan flight, they sing such beautiful songs they put Ireland to sleep for three days and nights.

Tales of transformation into swans likely refer to forgotten shamanic flights of consciousness, which are associated with the feminine path of magic, as the swan is the totem of the Goddess.

EIGHTEEN

Spirit Birds

Song of the Feminine Christ

Swan lyres were used by ancient Womb priestesses in their ecstatic feminine rites, dating back at least three thousand years. Spirit birds such as swans and doves were feminine symbols of the Great Mother and were often depicted in statues, altar icons, vases, and carvings in places of worship of a feminine deity. The idea of music and spirit birds was also entwined in ancient feminine traditions. In fact, the old English word *swan* comes from the proto-Germanic word *swanaz,* which means "singer." Priestesses and feminine spirit weavers used "swan songs" to journey to the Otherworld, to heal, to prophesize, to enchant, and to guide departed spirits home. Special harps and lyres carved with symbols of swans were used by these feminine sound shamans. In Celtic lore, myths recount how this otherworldly singing could alter consciousness, and in Greek traditions priestesses used their swan lyres and swan songs in ritual and ceremony. Likewise, priestesses in Egypt were renowned for their ability to use music to shape-shift consciousness, and Isis was depicted with swan wings. As the feminine wisdom ways were destroyed, this ancient magical sound practice disappeared, with only fragments of ancient vases and sculptures bearing witness to the tradition.

After discovering the magic feminine traditions connected to swan lyres and sacred music, Azra and I felt incredibly lucky to become guardians of a beautiful swan lyre with which to revive these ancient feminine traditions and reenchant the *swan songs* of mystical feminine consciousness.

The sound of the swan lyre transports us back in time and touches a deep place in the feminine soul. In 2015 we led a pilgrimage to France. Gathered in a small French church, which legends said was built over a Temple of Isis, our pilgrims played the swan lyre as an oracular instrument in devotion to Mary. On another occasion back in the United States, upon hearing the swan lyre, one woman was in tears, saying, "It's like I've been thirsting for this without knowing what it was." For those connected to feminine magic, these sounds are like a soul song.

To our knowledge the swan lyre that we became custodians of and use in ceremony is one of the first of its kind in the world to be used for ceremonial purpose as part of the feminine mysteries for at least a thousand years—if not longer. Its music is a swan song of a lost memory calling out. It reminds us of a time when women used sound magic to heal and awaken.

The Swan Lyre also has a beautiful finger labyrinth carved into her side and is adorned with crystals. Finger labyrinths help us calm our mind and open the mystical consciousness of our cerebellum before we play. Simply tracing our finger across the carved labyrinth path opens a magical doorway within, and so rather than us playing the swan, she can sing through us.

Spirit Birds of the Goddess

Birds are sacred to the feminine across many traditions. In India, the swan is sacred to the primordial goddess Saraswati (the great river), who is also goddess of the arts and is depicted playing a lute and riding a swan. In Greece, the swan is sacred to Aphrodite, and in the Celtic lands, the swan is sacred to the goddess Bride. In Egypt, the goose is sacred to Isis, and in the Semitic lands, the dove is associated with the feminine spirit of the Great Mother—later called the Holy Spirit in Christianity.

Around the world, spirit birds are a symbol of the Goddess—and a symbol of Womb priestesses and female Womb shamans who could fly the dream paths of spirit using magic, prayer, ritual dance, sacred sound, and incantation.

In Minoan and Mycenaean art, the bird is often a symbol of the Goddess. In Homer's *Odyssey,* the gods and goddesses are often depicted as shape-shifting spirit birds. Athena, the goddess of wisdom, is frequently portrayed as a holy spirit bird: "Thus having spoken, gray-eyed Athena departed, and as a bird she flew away, upwards."

At Knossos Palace in Crete, miniature terracotta columns with birds perched on top have been discovered—a common symbolic motif of the ascent of the kundalini, flying like a feminine spirit bird up the spinal column and ascending into the heavens of the magical glandular doorways of the crown. Similarly, in ancient Christian tradition, receiving the Holy Spirit of the dove described an initiation given by the Goddess into the divine powers of the cosmic kundalini.

In ancient Greece, birds are found with female figurines, and a terracotta seal from Zakro depicts an eagle-headed female shaman, her wings outstretched, dancing, with rounded breasts.

At the Shrine of Double Axes in Knossos, the bird goddess appears with upraised hands—a posture known as drawing down the moon or drawing down the cosmic kundalini. She is often depicted with a great headdress decorated with a bird—again showing the soul realization of feminine enlightenment. She is also mentioned on stone tablets as the dove goddess.

Bird lyres were often a part of the feminine mysteries, weaving the enchantment of sound with feminine awakening, often accompanied by the ritual dance of Womb priestesses.

In a terracotta group from Palaikastro, three women dance around a central female lyre player, and a spirit bird of feminine awakening lands before her, blessing the lyre player. Archaeologists have discovered three circular dancing platforms at Knossos (built before 1425 BCE) used for ecstatic trance dance and song to bring divine epiphanies and oracular insight.

These feminine ecstatic arts were once the heartland of the sacred Womb priestess and her prophetic healing powers.

Remembering these rituals is a spiritual archaeology of a lost feminine religion, whose priestesses and rites were forbidden by a patriarchal culture trying to destroy the feminine spirit.

Sacred Rites of the Ancient Womb Religion

These rites often emerged from the Neolithic Age, beginning in 8000 BCE, and the Bronze Age, beginning in 3500 BCE, and may harken back to much older ancient mystical rites that existed before the Ice Age.

By the Bronze Age, depictions of birds and lyres as sacred items was a common feature of Great Mother worship and the priests and priestesses who practiced her primordial religion.

In a chamber tomb excavated near Chania, Crete, archaeologists discovered a pyxis (a cylindrical clay box) dating from 1300–1250 BCE, showing a male figure with a seven-stringed lyre, taller than he is. To the left of the lyre are two horns of consecration, with a double axe standing in the middle. This iconography depicts the sacred image of the uterus, the life-bearing Great Womb with her majestic fallopian horns and central axis, the world cross, which was believed to be a shamanic portal to the spirit world.

As the long-robed musician plays, the priestess pours liquid offerings into a large jar—the feminine Holy Grail vessel. The jar stands between two double axes, symbol of the Womb, with sacred birds of kundalini awakening perched on top.

It was said that playing the magical lyre could call forth divine beings, who crossed the threshold in the form of spirit birds.

The sacred sound of the lyre also spoke to the ancestors across time and allowed them to travel the songlines to commune with the living and for the living to travel to the Underworld—the world of the dead—or, in Celtic tradition, the faerie world or Annwn where the use of the lyre or harp was also common.

Music was often used in birth and death rites, helping souls incarnate into this world. New souls journeyed on the back of a spirit bird, such as a stork or swan, or a swan barge or the barque of Isis. By these sacred songlines, souls could also return home, crossing the cervical threshold back to spirit.

On one end of the sarcophagus from Ayia Triada, two goddesses arrive for the dead in chariots drawn by griffins, as a bird accompanies them overhead. Lyre players are depicted playing their otherworldly instruments.

Swan Lyres of the Feminine Mysteries

One of the most significant bird symbols of the Great Mother Goddess is the swan—an icon of feminine womb enlightenment. At Knossos on Crete, a small alabaster lyre is decorated with a swan's head on each arm of the instrument. Slightly later, across the Aegean in the fourteenth century BCE, lyres have S-shaped arms and are frequently decorated with waterbirds.

Minoan seals show stylized bird lyres, and vases from seventh-century Smyrna show a longnecked bird above a lyre.

Depictions of religious rites show a female priestess in ceremonial dress standing on a sphinx, wearing a tall headdress bearing a large swan head. In a sculptural group from Bogazkoy in Turkey, a goddess is flanked by an attendant playing a bird-headed lyre. In the sanctuary of Artemis at Ephesos, excavated ivory swan heads are thought to belong to lyres.

Swan lyres called forth the spirit blessing of the Great Mother, who poured down her cosmic kundalini on the priests and priestesses who performed her rites. The sacred sound awakened the feminine shamanic gateway between the worlds so the Womb priestesses and shamans could fly the songlines of the Otherworld. This was one of the origins of the phrase *swan song.*

The song of the swan is returning, as the feminine Christ within awakens to restore cosmic primordial consciousness.

Resources

Carter, Jane B. "Ancestor Cult and the Occasion of Homeric Performance." Chap. 18 in *The Ages of Homer,* edited by Jane B. Carter and Sarah P. Morris. Austin: University of Texas Press, 1995.

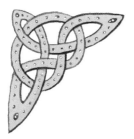

NINETEEN

Soul Fertility

Our Audacious Creativity

Within us is a creative spirit that is full of power, inspiration, and wisdom. Our creativity is full of passion, knowing, imagination, and a wild, wondrous audacity.

Our creativity can express through our art, but its true expression is through the work of art that is our everyday lives. This inner creativity guides us with magical fairy lights along the path. It asks us to live a creative life, to breathe into trust, to have deep and wild relatings. When we have hit rock bottom, our creative spirit brings us an elevator and presses up.

It gives us courage, passion, inspiration, insight, and the balm of true beauty. By connecting to our wild creative spirit, we create magical doorways where we have previously met only roadblocks. Our creativity is a magician, a sorceress of life.

Creativity lives by this truth: there is always a way. If there is not a visible path, then creativity forges one. If there is no way out, then creativity takes off the roof and flies. It asks us to imagine the unimaginable—that we are empowered creators, rebels of consciousness, spinners of fates, tellers of tales, birthers of dreams.

Creativity invites us into our ecstasy by awakening our inner sensual epiphanies and shouting at us from the bleachers when we are playing small and staying safe.

Its magical firepower sustains us even when everything around us has fallen.

The impulse to create, weave, paint, spin, dream, dance, tell stories, and imagine has been with us since the dawn of time—in fact this very impulse is our creator!

No one can take our creativity away from us because its passion lives deep inside us and is the fabric of our being. It is our superpower, our inner jewel, our savior.

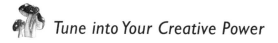 *Tune into Your Creative Power*

❍ Take a deep breath.

❍ Put your hands on your womb. Breathe into the fertile darkness.

❍ Ask to meet your own audacious creativity. What does it look like? How does it feel? What messages is it bringing for your life?

❍ What ideas or visions arise? Even if you feel lost, scared, tired, sad, overwhelmed, your creativity is still inside, alive, inspired—and it has a cunning plan! You can trust this voice.

❍ What hidden or forgotten desires can you feel in your heart? This creative impulse knows how to light you up and bring the magic of fire to your desires and powers of manifestation.

❍ Open to a sense of rooted trust. All your creative power asks of you is one thing. Trust. Actually, it will ask a second thing of you. Courage.

Your creative spirit will probably require you to dance with chaos—and teach you to laugh as you fumble your steps. Creativity loves audacity, and it nose-kisses those who fail valiantly. It loves to experiment with crazy ideas and thrives on "what if?"

Creativity is very spirited: it dares our inner hero or heroine to dream bolder. But it is also very serious and practical and imbued with the wisdom of common sense.

Sometimes its greatest magic lives in the smallest of details. It is how we cook a meal, how we make love, what we write in our journal, how we show up for life.

It flows through us in dreams, doodles, music, humming, nature walks, poems. It connects us more deeply into the web of life and our own humanity because life is creativity. It is the spirit to thrive, to find elegant solutions, to open to love and grow.

Creativity has nothing to do with success, perfection, money, status, technical ability, or external approval—in fact it will turn its nose up at such limited constraints.

This audacious spirit within us resonates to the sound of deep belly laughs, torrential tears of sorrow, vows of love, soul commitment, and the word *yes!*

It brings us the lightness of heart to carry on in the darkest of times.

Years ago, I was writing a book about the female president of Médicins Sans Frontières, whom I will call GG. MSF, also known as Doctors Without Borders, sent doctors and nurses to the most war-torn places of devastation to offer their medical support.

This woman was a living fireball of Audacious Creativity, and her stories inspired me with the indomitable spirit of humanity and what it truly took to live creatively.

I would like to share a few of these stories.

GG shared with me a story of a time when she was working with Mother Teresa in India. They had been traveling together in a car into the city to get some supplies. During this journey they happened to drive past a severe car accident involving a bus, which had happened only moments ago. They stopped the car to see if they could help. The scene was one of confusion and chaos: people were still trapped in the bus, and no one knew what to do. There was also the worry the bus would catch on fire. This being India, the emergency services would not be along any time soon.

Mother Teresa took stock of the situation and in full practical mode began galvanizing the crowds into a rescue team. Satisfied, Mother Teresa got back in the car to carry on with her day and the chores at hand, seemingly nonplussed. That is a saint in action.

The Holy Spirit is a creative energy; it prays practically with its feet and hands.

Another story touched me deeply and still brings me to tears now. GG was stationed in a refugee camp in Rwanda just after the genocide. To call this place hell would be too polite. She worked day in and day out in an emergency medical tent, in boiling heat, working with people whose lives and bodies had been decimated, where extreme suffering was a normal occurrence. The only thing that made this bearable was the incredible African nurses who she worked alongside. Always smiling, helpful, practical—their kindness and wisdom infused this place.

Every morning they would turn up for work on time, smiling, immaculate.

"How did they do it?" she would ask, as she walked around, tired, sweaty, stained.

She imagined they must ride in a bus from the nearest city every morning and return home on the same bus to a husband, family, food, washing facilities.

After work, she had a chance to talk to one of the nurses.

She was stunned by what she discovered.

These immaculate, smiling, inspiring nurses were also refugees.

Many had lost loved ones, sometimes their entire family. They had survived through the darkest of times. They lived in the camp, with squalor all around.

Often they had adopted orphaned children and cared for broods of over ten kids.

After working during the day, they returned at night to these families, looking after them, organizing them, spinning gold from their hearts and clothing the children in love.

It was more than a miracle. It was magic—the creative magic of the human spirit.

For me, these were divine mothers in nurses' outfits. They are the embodiment of creativity—a force that survives and extends its glow to warm and light up others.

Hopefully, most of us will not have to find our creative spirit under such severe circumstances. But we all have our own inner places of devastation and desolation calling out to us, and we can bring our own creative spirit to bless and heal them.

When we feel defeated and say, "It's not possible, I can't, I give up," our creativity whispers sonnets to us and sings melodies saying, "There is a way."

If you can paint it, sing it, sound it, cry it, dream it, feel it—you can birth it.

There is a way.

TWENTY

PRIMORDIAL DEVOTION

How the Feminine Prays

I pray with the primordial rivers of life flowing through my awakened body.

I pray as a mystical doorway opens in my inner womb, leading out into a vaulted cathedral of feminine consciousness flowing infinitely from the Divine Mother's Womb.

I pray as my body begins to transform into a cosmic gateway and the void dissolves my mud-drenched pain into roots and fresh shoots and touches me with her starlit fingertips of love.

I pray as my womb becomes a bridge for all that has left to return.

I pray with my grief, with my sorrow, with my heart shattered open into a million fragments, as if the first primordial burst of creation is still reverberating inside.

I pray with my heart, even when it is closed, frightened, confused, and afraid.

I pray because I am fragile. I have been broken. I cannot do this alone.

I pray because I am immeasurably strong and ferocious. I pray with howls for the suffering of the world. I pray with the fury of forgotten wrath.

I pray when I have no more prayers left and hopelessness is with me.

I pray when it is all smashed on the floor and cannot be fixed.

I pray with fangs and claws and the power of fire-forged volcanic ash. I pray to digest all the pain deep into the soil of my belly and birth out wildflowers.

I pray because there is a fire in me that cannot go out, which lights every dark night.

I pray as I prepare food and boil water and clean toilets. I pray with dirty rags and beautiful jewels. I pray with beauty, and I pray with the ugliness of all that is unsaid.

I pray with laughter and birdsong and forest floors. I pray with the softness.

I pray with tree roots and earthworms and fur. I pray with the rain and the snow. I pray with my touch, and I pray with my love. I pray with my consecrated womb.

I pray with the blood that floods from the inner luminosity of my celestial mansion.

We are the whores and the holy ones, honored and scorned, wild and unborn.

Our prayers are the song of the universe calling us home.

Weaving
Our Healing

TWENTY-ONE

WILD FEMININE

Dreaming with Mother Earth

We are feeling an immense birthing energy flowing into the world in our times. This energy surges in waves of crystal light flowing in from the galactic center, which scientists have confirmed appears to be intelligent and communicating with us.

Earth is a sentient being who is our primordial mother. Whether we are conscious of it or not, we have a deeply intimate relationship with her elements. On a physical level, her food and waters become our body. Without her, we could not live. On a spiritual level, Earth loves to share a conscious, co-creative relationship with us. She feels our joy, our pleasure, our pain; she knows our desires and hopes.

Our ancestors dedicated much of their spiritual lives to nurturing a deep relationship with the natural world that surrounded them and the cycles that turned the wheel of time, in a seasonal and celestial birth-death-rebirth cycle.

With this mystical connection, they celebrated a living mystery play with the land, through ritual, ceremony, prayer, celebration, vision quests, feasting, and fasting. This created a dream time of communion for humans and their environment.

Earth is asking us to redream this connection, and rewild the world.

Earth needs our help. She is calling to us.

 Keys to Earth-Remembering Activism

- ☽ Follow the moon cycles; buy a moon calendar; go outside in the moonlight.
- ☽ Honor your own moon cycles with ritual: offer your blood back to Earth.
- ☽ Celebrate and connect to the turning season—equinox, solstice, imbolc.
- ☽ Become aware of the plants, flowers, trees, and animals in your local habitat.
- ☽ Grow herbs and plants—even in a window box if you don't have a garden.
- ☽ Take five minutes a day to commune with Earth: listen and ask what she needs.
- ☽ Protect your local forests, rivers, and animal habitats with community action.
- ☽ If you live in a city, find ways to bring nature back, such as city gardens.

⟫ Connect to the spirit of the land. Can you sense its unique personality?

⟫ Gather together in circles; sing, dance, celebrate, and share meals together.

⟫ Be bold; hold a new vision; trust your magical faerie knowing.

> *We are bleeding at the roots because we are cut off from the earth and sun and stars.*
>
> D. H. LAWRENCE, "A PROPOS OF
> *LADY CHATTERLEY'S LOVER*"

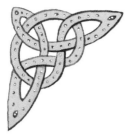

TWENTY-TWO

Underworld Journey

The Descending Path

*Light is the left hand of darkness
and darkness the right hand of light.
Two are one, life and death, lying
together like lovers in kemmer,
like hands joined together,
like the end and the way.*

URSULA K. LE GUIN,

THE LEFT HAND OF DARKNESS

Female power frightens people, and as a culture we vilify the very power that birthed us, which brings fertility, life, and growth to our planet. Every year, on October 31, Samhain (which was once celebrated as the Celtic New Year in the Northern Hemisphere), we begin to descend into the Underworld. Even mentioning the word *underworld* is overwhelming for some people, who believe it represents evil. Yet in ancient traditions the Underworld was understood to be the Womb of the Earth, the Womb of the Goddess, the womb of woman. It is the dark fertility of the soil that all plants and beings arise from and which they descend to upon death. The plants we eat, which sustain our life, grow from the Underworld realms of Earth. Babies grow in the underworld darkness of our wombs before birthing into the light. Many religions, even patriarchal, use this as a central metaphor for their beliefs. Except that we have forgotten the feminine cycles of birth-death-rebirth. We fear the darkness of the Underworld, which is now also a lost realm of our psyche, where all our deepest pain—starting from our time in the womb—is stored. We need to reclaim our descending, underworld feminine power.

From time out of mind, people took journeys into the Underworld to experience a rebirth into the light and to unite the fertilizing darkness and the light of creation. The Underworld was almost always a symbolic space of a magical womb, a dark container of birth and emergence.

Even the Bible—which is full of ancient wisdom—describes this shamanic journey, saying in Ephesians 4:9–10 (New International Version): "What does 'he ascended' mean except that he also descended to the lower, earthly regions? He who descended is the very one who ascended higher than all the heavens, in order to fill the whole universe." Jesus followed the feminine pathway of a descent into the Underworld, or the earth womb, now hell—once taken by goddesses like Inanna and the European goddess Hel, or Holle—so that he could root his awakening and ascend into the light.

In faerie tradition the Underworld was accessed by a faerie mound, and entering the realm of the faeries was often a terrifying, magical, life-changing voyage into a liminal space of transformation. When people emerged back out, many years may have passed, and their friends or family either didn't recognize them or they had already passed away. Symbolically, this encodes the knowing that those who are rebirthed from the Underworld womb of Mother Earth, from the magical realms of the Mother, can rarely fit back into normal cultural systems.

This experience of quantum death and rebirth is key to many world traditions. We descend into the unknown and let go of an old version of ourselves, which can feel like a terrifying ordeal, so that something new emerges. This new version of ourselves can feel like a changeling.

This call of the faeries to their magical realm is described poetically by W. B. Yeats:

Where the wave of moonlight glosses
The dim gray sands with light,
Far off by furthest Rosses
We foot it all the night,
Weaving olden dances
Mingling hands and mingling glances
Till the moon has taken flight;
To and fro we leap
And chase the frothy bubbles,
While the world is full of troubles
And anxious in its sleep.
Come away, O human child!
To the waters and the wild
With a faery, hand in hand,
For the world's more full of weeping than you can understand.

WILLIAM BUTLER YEATS, FROM "THE STOLEN CHILD"

As the poem intimates, our journeys to the Underworld often begin on rivers of tears, and the weight of the world's weeping as we flow down into the place that nourishes the root of life. We close the door on the light for a while. We enter into our psychic chrysalis, a quantum chamber of metamorphosis, so we can emerge back out in a new state of consciousness. In other traditions this realm is the darkness of bardo in Buddhist teachings or Du'at in the magical Egyptian traditions. In Ireland the keening women (*bean chainte*) wailed during grief rituals calling for the banshee—the faerie woman—to come and attend to the soul entering the Otherworld. A cry of the banshee indicated either a physical death or a spiritual death and rebirth within the faerie realm. The banshee carries all the tools of the ancient goddess traditions, such as a mirror and comb, and is often to be found near water or a river, combing her hair and lamenting.

Tune into your deep, dark inner space. Can you feel the cry of the banshee inside?

TWENTY-THREE

Witch Wound

Reclaiming Our Wisdom

As women rise into their power, we face all that once held us down.

We meet everything that has shamed us, blamed us, judged us.
We face the long shadow of "The Inquisitor" in all the forms he or she takes.
It looms large in the dark of our nightmares, our anxiety, our self-doubt.
We recognize its brutal energy—even if it shines bright as an artificial light.

And sometimes . . . we buckle under its burden.

We fold our power up like an old rag and stuff it back under the bed.
We live as if our incandescence deserves the death penalty.
We forget we were born to fly.

When I meet this energy, my body goes into primal shock.
I feel like I am living the wound of the witches again.
I'm aware that only a few hundred years ago women were burnt on the stake.
From this ancestral and past-life PTSD, it's as if I am recapitulating the past
times of losing my family, my beloved, my babies to this persecution.
I feel a deep cry in my womb-heart where she has closed tight in shock.

I remember as a child my mother telling me about the Inquisition, and we
would be horrified to imagine what it would be like to be the witches on
the hour of their death, approaching the flames. Mum would say that some
chose it rather than recant. "How could they be so brave?" she would ask.
"How could they endure it?"

As a teenager I had a brief flirtation with the Christian religion.
I told my mum that I wanted her to go to heaven, not hell.
She told me to tidy my room and that nature was heaven.

The vicar came to visit one night, and Mum wouldn't let him in. She kept him on the step, in the cold dark of the night, and made him account for the Inquisition and the lives of millions of women. He took it quite well, and after Mum had worked her way through a lecture on the worst atrocities the church had inflicted on the world, he apologized, and then she let him in for a cup of tea.

In Europe alone, there is a still a deep psychic scar of thousands of years of religious wars. And the effects of these wars have been spat out across the world.

Religions claiming "The Truth" have often burned people at the stake of their righteousness.

Cathars in France: persecuted, tortured, murdered.
Catholics in England: persecuted, tortured, murdered.
Protestants, Huguenots, Jews, Muslims, Gnostics: killed.
Wise women, midwives, herbalists: burnt.
Anyone considered different or other: targeted.
Anglicans in England imprisoned for lighting candles and singing hymns.
People across the world colonized, enslaved, and persecuted.

What is this madness? What is this "collective inquisition"?
It does not belong exclusively to the Catholic Church.
It lives inside us, like a deadly, contagious virus.

And even now, in our modern world, this "inquisition" goes strong.
It thrives on internet forums, in schools, in relationships.
It thrives in politics, in workplaces, even in "spiritual" circles.
Be small, shut up, do as you're told—or else, it says.
It wants to own, to bully, to dominate, to possess.
It threatens others with its sword of righteousness.
It claims our soul as its own.

But only if we let it.

Our fear gives it power.

We can choose love, time and time again, no matter what.

Even if we are figuratively burnt at the stake—in whatever form that takes for us in this modern world—this is the wound of the witches within us. Much as we would like to hide our light to avoid its terrifying shadows, our feminine power will ask that we meet it and reclaim what was lost.
As we root into the knowing that our voice needs to rise and be heard, we become a grail bearer for that which serves and protects all forms of life.

My womb reminds me her power flows deep and can never be destroyed.
I remember:
I cannot live with my heart closed.
I cannot live without following my feminine soul.
I cannot live without claiming my feminine power.
I cannot live without giving everything to this great love I have experienced.

So I sit back with the unimaginable horror of that question my mum had asked:
How do you face that fire?
I understand that in some mysterious way, she already knew in her bones. Her body still remembered, infused with the cellular soul-memories of those past events.
Maybe she was asking my body too, who also remembered, deep, deep down.

So I prayed to the Divine Mother to help me.
I felt all my fear ignite in those flames.
The Divine Mother said, "Let's walk into the fire together."

I give myself to the Great Remembering. I leave no wound without balm.

There is a feeling so deep, so essential, held in the fathomless depths of the feminine, that you can burn it a million times at the stake . . . and you will never extinguish it . . . it is the same force by which even the greatest city, the most powerful civilization will fall to ruin and be reclaimed by nature in time, dissolved completely by the living tendrils of fresh green shoots, in innocence renewed.

ORACLE RECEIVED FROM THE WOMB LYRE BY SEREN BERTRAND, 2012

TWENTY-FOUR

Shadow Healing

Rebirthing the Feminine

We are rebirthing our hearts for love . . .

Feminism, the women's liberation movement, started unofficially when Mary Magdalene and her goddess of love took a sneaky back door into the boy's club of the Bible and began officially in the West when the female Christian mystic of the fourteenth century, Julian of Norwich, suggested with visionary aplomb that Christ might be the Cosmic Mother. It then continued with Mary Wollstencraft's pioneering "A Vindication for the Rights of Women" in 1792 and abolitionist and women's rights advocate Sojourner Truth's searing call for equality for *all* women in the 1800s, and progressed into the 1920s with Emmeline Pankhurst and the suffragettes winning the right for women to vote. Finally it blossomed into the 1970s as women burnt their bras on the pyre of equality, and various new streams of feminism emerged.

For many women in the West, we had the right to vote, to work, to buy, to have sex, to control our own fertility, to have same-sex marriages, to have abortions (only just), to have artificial conceptions, to divorce, to becomes priests (priestesses were still too scary). We even had the right to be legally raped by our own husbands (previously not recognized as a crime). Heck, the Catholic Church even admitted, grudgingly, that we had souls.

Yet this evolutionary thread is a living creature that transforms for each epoch.

In some circles, it feels as if feminism is undergoing its own version of a shamanic death and rebirth—its own descent into Inanna's fertile underworld to renew. Right now, there is a new "feminine-ism" birthing that embraces a woman's deep feminine essence.

This is a female power that does not need to put on trousers to prove its worth. This is a feminine power that inhabits itself and its desires with ease and without apology, that embodies both fierceness and softness without paradox, that luxuriates in the sensual potentials of sexuality and earthly communion. This feminine essence is magnetic, and centered in the magic of the body.

 ## Feminism and Her Broken Heart

Growing up in a traditional working-class environment—where only a generation before my grandmother had addressed her husband as "lord" and in my mother's generation women were still not legally allowed to get a mortgage—feminism was a lifeline away from a life of laundry and lost dreams and gave me a way to vision the kind of life I wanted to live.

Yet in my desire to make a radical departure from the patriarchal world of fear, despair, suffering, poverty, control, and drudgery I saw around me, I also took a radical departure from men, from viewing and honoring the masculine as part of me.

In leaving a broken system behind, I had unintentionally left half of my heart too. I had not understood that underneath the broken system was a broken heart.

I also left part of my feminine soul behind. I had been granted the freedom to become a man in a woman's body, to embody the dictates of a production, goal-oriented system that could never rest, recline, and surrender into exquisite bliss.

I loved men, I had relationships with men, I longed for men, I admired men—strange creatures that they were to me. I also subconsciously hated them, blamed them, belittled them, felt angry toward them and disempowered by them, withheld from them.

When I looked around to find the embodiment of the sacred masculine—courage, compassion, strength, commitment, protection—I could easily find it . . . expressed in the strong females I saw around me. My friends, my sisters.

We would collectively complain: Where are all the good men? The heroes? Yet I had failed to ask: Where is my wild femininity? My devotional heart? It had closed somewhere along the way to protect itself from hurt.

 ## Kissing the Hurt of Hate

The fissure in my heart began to open when in the space of a week two people said that I hated men. It wasn't said as an accusation, just as an observation of fact, as if it would be naturally evident to me.

Yet it wasn't obvious to me . . .

I didn't hate men! They tasted good on a slice of toast or washed down with wine. Yes, of course they were remedial in some ways, but didn't they have smaller brains or something? Hadn't their good sense been diverted into muscle?

And weren't they single-handedly, or single-penisedly, raping and destroying the world and responsible for everything? Oh God, now I was in the collective wound. What was this place? So much rage and anguish—and such deep grief.

So it began to dawn on me. I did hate men. I was angry. I was judgmental. But I'd kept it all wrapped up in such a nice, sweet smile that even I hadn't noticed it.

And then I allowed myself to descend into that great wound, that collective pit.

I lowered myself down gently at first, half screaming, part numb, to discover what I would find there. I passed through my mother's pain and all the pain of the mothers before her and into the collective scream, frozen, like a gothic expressionist painting. This was the hell within my feminine ancestry, forgotten, abandoned.

What I discovered was that I didn't hate men. *I hated me.*

I hated all the pain, the fear, the grief, the betrayal that was living within me, still unexpressed, and the unworthiness, the repressed anger it generated within me.

I hated all the looping storylines of anguish, abuse, abandonment that had been told endlessly down my epigenetic DNA, until I took guardianship for this generation's inheritance of loss, overwhelmed, overburdened, lost, confused, piteously trapped in this silent collective scream, that had to get out, had to be voiced.

What did this hate want? What balm did this bitterness need? I asked.

Love, it answered. Love. Sweetness. Softness. Kindness. To be held in safe arms.

In this velvet darkness of embrace I found Ereshkigal, the Mesopotamian goddess of the dead, a straight-talking Moll Flanders of the Underworld, with her heart of gold and feet of clay.

There is more. She told me. Go deeper.

So I lowered myself deeper into this seemingly endless pit, now curious as to what I'd find down there. What could be more than this? Down I went, through layers.

Here I met the pain of the masculine. Of my father, of his father. Of all the fathers. The grief, the loss, the shame, the longing. I met the boy children, their penises cut, their souls severed, their feelings torn away from their innocent gentle hearts.

I met the men I had loved, the men I would love. The man who was half of me.

In this moment I became Isis.

My anguished lament pierced the ice.

My soul cried out to the furthest reaches of the universe.

I will never stop searching for you, beloved.

I will re-member you and the love we shared.

I was crying for my father, for my beloved, for all men. They were all one.

Returning Home to Love

My hate was the frozen pain of a broken heart. As it melted, love flowed again.

I discovered that if I was to relove myself I had to include my other half. There was a woman and a man that needed liberating within and without.

I thanked feminism for giving the pain of my mothers a voice. I thanked feminism for all the work she had done for me, and all the important work still left undone, all the stories still waiting patiently to be voiced, heard, redeemed, liberated. I thanked her for all the rights claimed, lives saved, the cases advocated, the work to come.

But for me, this thank you was also a good-bye of sorts.

I had taken my feminism into the Underworld with me and she had rebirthed. I was no longer lit up by anger; I was on fire with love.

My feminism now wore a soft shawl of stars and rode wild and naked in magical moonlight vistas and offered lingering, loving kisses of redemption to all the frightened hard angles of oppression she found before her. She was feminine.

Now on those forbidden moonlit nights, making love with my beloved, I open into the uncanny knowing and feeling that I am making love with a part of myself who has returned home to me, as I have returned home to my true self.

That which was torn apart is being slowly, tenderly, stitched back together.

TWENTY-FIVE

LAMENTATIONS

The Shamanic Pathway of Grief

Watching my father die was a transformational experience, like witnessing a reverse birthing process, where the doors of the spirit world are flung right open and light streams through—a light so intense and searing it tears a rip in the fabric of time and place and breaks your heart open into a million dazzling, devastated pieces.

A person you love, and whose body gifted you your body, is leaving.
It is like being on the edge of a cosmic black hole and watching someone fly. I felt profoundly altered in consciousness, ecstatic at times, between worlds. Yet I had to turn back and return to this realm. I had to say good-bye.

Grief is the gift that helps us ground and integrate these deep shamanic experiences.

I next saw my father laid out in a sustainable woven basket coffin at the undertakers. His face looked like wax; it was as if it were a resemblance of him but not quite him. He had on his best suit and tie, and they had combed his hair nicely.

I placed cherished amulets in the coffin with him—his favorite dressing gown, some family photos—and then sat on the gray carpet and wept. I didn't want to leave. There was no otherworldly experience this time. It was very real, very fragile, very painful. The only words that would come out were, "I love you, Dad. Thank you." I kept repeating them like a prayer mantra. It was as if a whole life lay inside them.

Grief is oceanic; it comes in tides. It ebbs and flows. It surprises you with immense tidal waves that loom from nowhere and crash down on your heart. Sometimes it is perfectly still, like moonlight shimmering on a black ocean—remote and abyss deep. Sometimes it flows like warm honey, resonating with laughter and tender memories. Sometimes it is nowhere to be seen, as if the heart is made of forgetful ancient rock.

Sometimes you think "I'm over it," and grief gently takes your hand to remind you.

Grief takes time and patience. It lives at odds with our fast-paced world.

Grief itself is very patient. If we push it away, it waits. It takes years to unfold. We have so much grief patiently waiting on us, buried like seeds in our heart. We can't force our way to it either or get it over with. It has its organic way with us. It will not allow us to fast-forward or to escape its time-honored labyrinth path.

Grief invites us to "wait in God," as author Sue Monk Kidd puts it. This is a waiting that is pregnant with the healing power of deep night. We offer ourselves over to God to hold us. We wait together for the light to return—while making ourselves comfortable inside the darkness of the womb of grief. We make ourselves OK with not being OK. There are no quick fixes, no spiritual theories or reassurances that can cure it, or wrap it up with a nicely made bow. It just is. It roots us down into the Underworld, like it or not, and begins to restructure the fabric of our psyche.

It does not take a week or a month or a year or three years. It is timeless.

The last time I hugged my dad was on the day of my legal wedding. We had celebrated our spiritual wedding a few days earlier, inside a red ribbon circle threaded round a grove of trees, surrounded by our kin in a beautiful Welsh valley.

Three days later we got married legally in a register office. Only my mum and dad attended as witnesses. I saw my dad cry as we placed our hands on the Bible and made our vows. As far as my dad was concerned, this was our "proper" wedding. As a traditional northern man, *legally married* were the magic words. His job was done.

We left in a rush, eager to begin the long drive up to Scotland for our honeymoon. I hugged him and said good-bye. I wish I had spent time with that hug. I wish I'd etched that hug on my heart and made sure I'd said, "I love you." But I can't remember. How was I to know this would be the last time I hugged him like this?

I'd given him a big bear hug so many times it was as if there were an endless supply.

I did not know this would be the final one . . .

The last time I saw him he was so frail and hooked up to so many tubes I could not hug him. I sat by him, I held his hand, I kissed his cheek, I stroked his forehead, I fussed with the blankets on his bed, I got his favorite soup. But I could not hug him.

A month after he died, in a vivid dream my father appeared to me. He was wearing his everyday white shirt, straining a bit round the waist. He was vividly, in every inch, in every little detail I had ever known, my dad—I remembered it all at once.

I told him how sad I was that I had not had one last hug.

He said, "Don't be daft," and then gave me a big bear hug as I wept in his arms. This was a hug from heaven. I discovered that there is no such thing as the end. Grief is a peculiar thing; it is the secret sister of love. It melts us and merges us back into the heart of creation, if we allow it to. Its fountain of tears are crystals of love.

This shamanic grief that leads us to the mystery of infinite love is not a sentimental grief. It does not paper overs the cracks of truth with idealization and forgetfulness or transfigure the dead into a false picture of perfection. Instead, it honors the truth of life—complex, messy, hurtful, confusing, contradictory. Shamanic grief is a love that has become so spacious and timeless that it also includes the hurt and the hate. This is the incredible power of grief: its awesome cosmic rivers flow through our hearts with such devastating impact that all the hurt places are also taken up in its immense torrent and whooshed downstream into the deepest roots of our hearts for healing and restoration. Often death is the start of a deeper reconciliation.

My father was funny, honest, wise, loving, and one of a kind, truly northern bred. He was also patriarchal, obnoxious, deeply annoying. He loved me. And he hurt me.

Grief is the deepest love that includes all of this in its arms. Love is big enough.

On the one-year anniversary of my father's death, I received a Facebook message from him. Yes. You read that correctly, although your conscious mind may be scrambling. Mine certainly was. He sent a message, which contained a black background, like the dark infinity of the void, with a womb symbol in the center. Later on, I discovered that this triskele disc was identical to an old Buddhist symbol for reaching nirvana.

My no-nonsense, nonspiritual, cynical father was sending spiritual messages to me.

I could almost hear his Yorkshire-toned voice. "Death is the end? Don't be daft."

Grief is the bridge that extends between us. Grief is the infinity of love.

And I would still give anything for one last hug in this world.

TWENTY-SIX

Soft Power

The Magic of Vulnerability

Healing and reclaiming our open, receptive power . . .

Vulnerability is soft resilience. It is a healthy psychic tissue, supple and responsive, soft and fluid, and its power comes from its openness and trust.

All human beings by their original nature are vulnerable. We are sensitive, biological, soulful creatures who can be wounded. We can cry, bleed, hurt, die—but we are also soft, open, receptive. We are holy grails for the love currents of universal flow.

Healthy vulnerability is destroyed when we experience trauma. Our boundaries become barriers, our defense mechanisms become armies, and our softness becomes a shell of protection. Or we mistake lack of discernment for openness.

When our vulnerability has been wounded, we become fragile.
What was once soft becomes brittle, what was supple feels breakable.
The paradox is when we are fragile, we appear very hard.

Accepting Our Fragility

In our fragility, we are afraid of our feelings, our vulnerability, our need, our fear, our weakness. After all, these are the soft places we were once wounded in.

126

We have to get tough, independent, go it alone.
We erect hard walls around us.
We retreat into the mind.

Accepting our fragility helps us return to our healthy vulnerability. By consciously knowing what needs holding, we can release our unconscious protections.

And there is no easy fix or Band-Aid for those fragile places. No empower-ment pep talk, no reassurance, no spiritual reframe. It is devastating behind that broken glass. It is hard to know how to pick up the pieces and reweave the threads.

Often we can only hold the broken pieces in our hands and weep.

But by gathering the pieces and grieving we begin the healing.

 Our Original Wholeness

This reweaving, this remembering, is the call of the Goddess.
She who birthed us, who holds the creative blueprints, can rebirth us too.

Our fragility is like a lost child who can be held by our own mother instincts.

There is a light that shines through the broken pieces of our hearts to guide us. The magic of vulnerability holds the body-memory of our origi-nal wholeness.

Humanity has never been more fragile than now, as we stand on the brink of an ecological and planetary disaster, mirrored by our own inner disaster zones.

We need to call forth the power of softness.
To accept we are fragile and breakable.
To accept our world has already broken.
To begin creating the holding space needed for healing.

Healing Journey to Love

The deep restoration of our soul begins when we can form relationships from our wise and healthy vulnerability, gently peeling away the masks in a safe, holistic way—opening back to interconnection, while honoring our own natural boundaries.

We can also thank the hard walls that kept our incredible fragility protected for so long.

We can mourn the knowing that our strength was often forged in the cauldron of our most broken places and was the only means and way we had to survive.

From the beautiful vulnerability and wisdom of our big heart, we can now place our swan wings of compassion around our own inner fragility and nurse the broken heart of the world, as we walk together on our healing journey back to the wholeness of love.

TWENTY-SEVEN

HEALING HANDS

Opening Your Heart

Our hands are where the loving, trusting heart energy flows out so we can connect with the world and other people. If we love or like someone, we instinctively touch them with our hands. The energy of power and aggression also flows through the hands. When we are angry or tense, we instinctively clench our fists. When we feel threatened, we instinctively push someone away. If we feel scared, upset, or hurt, heart energy gets blocked in our hands. If we feel angry or threatened but feel powerless to express our aggression, then the energy traps in our hands and becomes a trauma signature. This is the same way our toes connect to the womb and hold tension, and we often describe moments of intense shame as being toe-curling.

Here are some exercises to help liberate the energy in the hands:

 ### Healing Hands, Open Heart

☽ Visualize light flowing from your heart, through your hands, through your fingers, and flowing out of your fingertips in threads of light.

☽ Play with dancing and weaving and spiraling your hands, visualizing these beautiful threads of light dancing too.

☽ Dance like this for five to ten minutes and hopefully your hands will get very hot and alive.

☽ Place your hands on your heart or womb or a part of your body you feel needs healing. Allow the heat, warmth, and light of the energy in your hands to flow into your body.

Releasing Trauma: Unclenching the Fist

❧ Sit quietly and breathe into the center of your hands; keep focusing your awareness in the center of your palms until you start to feel a heat there. Allow any feelings that come up.

❧ Keep your breath and awareness focused on the middle of your palms and now slowly clench your fists. How does it feel?

❧ Now very slowly open your hands. Go as slowly as you can, feeling the energy in the fists. Gently focus your awareness on the movement, not making it be anything, just allowing your primal self to move you. How does it feel to have your palms and fingers fully open?

❧ Now very slowly—as slowly as you can go—clench your fists again.

❧ Keep going like this for five minutes; allow any feelings or sensations, such as trembling, to come up. Afterward, sit for a few moments and breathe into the center of each palm.

❧ During the day keep checking in with how your hands feel. Notice how you hold them. Are they tense? Are you unconsciously clenching them? Are they stiff? Or do they feel disassociated? Is it hard to feel any energy or sensations there? Breathe and connect the energy in your hands to your arms, your shoulders, and heart.

❧ If you feel you need to make pushing movements, push on a heavy object. Or simply bring your hands into prayer position at your heart and breathe.

> *Consider the holiness of your hands. They are how you do your work on this earth; they are a microcosm of the hands of the Goddess, and can change the world as easily as hers can.*
> DIANNE SYLVAN, THE BODY SACRED

TWENTY-EIGHT

MOTHERLINE MAGIC

Healing Our Maternal Legacy

Jungian analyst Marion Woodman wrote a brilliant book in the mid-1990s called *Leaving My Father's House: A Journey to Conscious Femininity*. In it, Marion weaves together three women's stories, and using a European fairy story as a backbone to the narrative, she explores how women have to leave the "house that patriarchy built" within their own psyche and what that might mean or look like.

Now, more than twenty years later, there is a new healing cry within the feminine psyche.

Reflecting on it, it feels like I was kicked out of my father's house, with a swift foot to the ass, for too many revolutionary ideas about what women are and could be.

Yet there is still a huge, foreboding house within my psyche that the patriarchy built. This is the father's house our mother built. Its roots live deeper, more entangled.

This patriarchal edifice was created by our mothers, built brick by brick in the only way she knew how, as her mother had taught her, placed upon foundation stones forged from ancestral materials and memories. Cemented with guilt and shame.

It has the feel of Amityville, one of those terrifying haunted houses of fifties American films, which take the cozy dream of the nuclear family home

and cast it in darkness. It brings forward the hidden menace lurking behind respectable curtains.

I needed to leave the house she built, filled with the inhaled toxic fumes of repressed self-loathing and oppression.

And this is more difficult . . . because she is my mother. I grew in her body, her blood became my bones, her milk became my blood, she was the world and the Mother. How could I survive, leaving behind the false womb of her world?

In a way her house feels like my house.
So I am leaving behind who I thought "I" was.
I am vacating an entire feminine ideological structure to birth a new one.
And this is scary: it is the walk through the valley of death . . . and rebirth.

Right now, as a collective of women, we are journeying this together. We are leaving our mother's house so we can build the Mother's Temple.

There is no written map, no directions, other than our inner sensing.
It calls us into a radical trust of what we feel to be true within our bodies.
It calls for us to reject a false set of criteria we have been unwittingly given.
There are no guarantees and likely no approval or validation coming our way.
Instead, we are giving ourselves our own permission and self-approval.
We are digging in deep to find the inner ground to support us.

All about us, swirling high like hungry vultures, are the voices of those that live in the father's house our mother built. They can even be our sisters, our friends.

The reality is that there is, and has been, no true expression of fully conscious femininity for thousands of years on Earth. Women are the product of a broken world, where feminine values are destroyed, derided, raped, and exploited.

The maternal ancestral baggage is more like an avalanche than a suitcase.

Psychology shows that the most common effect of living under any form of abusive regime, overt in the physical world or subtle in the emotional realms, is that the victim takes on the value system of the abuser to survive. To do this, they even think they believe in this value system and that it is native to them.

From this place of conditioned certainty, they make sure to pass these values on.

As a child, the person we learn from and whom we emulate is the mother. We grow and develop our sense of self by a process of mirroring.

But what do we see? "Mirror, mirror on the wall, who is the fairest of them all?"

We are reflected values that objectify the feminine, strip her of her wild primal essence. Values that set women against women, fighting and competing for their survival.

In the mirror we see a mother who has been conditioned to be small, tight, not too loud, not too much, not too sexual, yet just sexually pleasing enough—like a pretty dessert that can be devoured by patriarchal structures, without causing indigestion.

Or we see a mother who has given up, broken, vacating her feminine being completely. Filled with the unspoken bitterness of drudgery and the hate it brings.

If the mothers of this world have been creating from a center of unconscious femininity, burdened with a historical pain-body of rape, ridicule, poverty, abandonment, submission, servitude, betrayal, mistrust, disconnection, then is it any surprise that we have inherited a world of loss, confusion, pain, fear?

Leaving the father's house our mother built means leaving behind our own inherited and conditioned sense of what it means to be a woman and what we need to be or do to be safe, accepted, loved. It means facing the opposites of those. It means expressing ourselves in ways that may not be liked. It means we may not survive in a man's world—or in a woman's world created in the image of patriarchy. We will have to find a new world within us and create from there.

But from the intense living gold forged by this navigation of the inner wasteland of feminine abandonment, a new realm emerges, a magical queendom within.

This grail journey means we will face our own fears that locked us in this safe house—and also the maternal ancestral pain that molded every brick, right down to the foundation stones. Bringing it down can be earth shattering, psyche shattering.

As it deepens, it also brings a heart-shattering compassion for our mother, for all mothers—and for the way we have mothered, with our own inheritance of loss.

This emerging conscious femininity is revelatory, almost apocalyptic; it has psychic blood on its hands. Yet this blood is that of menstruation. It is also deeply creative and powerful. It remembers the myths that say moon blood births new worlds.

There are many ways we can find to escape from this house that has imprisoned us. That has bricked us in, like virgin-sacrifices of old, into a soul-deadened structure.

Yet it is also as simple as leaving a note, closing the door, and walking out . . .

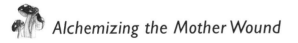 Alchemizing the Mother Wound

Explore your relationship to the internalized mother wound with these two lists outlining how this wound shows up in our lives when it is not yet healed, and how it feels when we have alchemized it into the *mother blessing*—granting us soul beauty and freedom in our being. You can journal your responses to each of the prompts on the list, or explore movement or sound in the vibration of the mother's *temple* compared to inside the mother's house.

The Interior Decor of the Father's House Our Mother Built

☽ Goodness means being thoughtful, nice, and kind.

☽ Female power is small, thin, artificially beautiful, perfect.

☽ Your anger is dangerous and harmful.

- ☽ Speaking your truth is unfair to others.

- ☽ Your sexual energy needs to be controlled.

- ☽ Your sexual energy needs to be sold or manipulated.

- ☽ It is more important to be normal than to be happy.

- ☽ Your clothes, possessions, achievements define you.

The Sacred Altar in the Mother's Temple You Built

- ☽ Goodness is the free flowing of your life force.

- ☽ Female power is rooted within your own body.

- ☽ Your anger is the roar of freedom and release.

- ☽ Speaking your truth creates inner harmony.

- ☽ Your sexual energy is pure, wild, free.

- ☽ Your sexual energy is sovereign to you.

- ☽ Happiness is being true to yourself.

- ☽ Your inner sense of value comes from self-love.

TWENTY-NINE

Yoni Temple

Healing Sacred Feminine Rituals

Can you feel something shifting in the collective consciousness? We are in the middle of an incredible renaissance of feminine wisdom.

Looking around, it becomes clear that this wisdom is downloading into our consciousness on an unprecedented scale, calling women back to their sacred center: their womb, the seat of the feminine power of creative manifestation.

For too long the feminine wisdom ways have been forgotten, buried, destroyed. The self-care rituals and feminine pathway initiations have been discarded by a culture that has sought to devalue and destroy the very power that birthed it.

The sacred traditions of our distant ancestors, which taught how to nurture, care for, protect, and awaken the womb, are no longer passed to us at menarche.

Instead, most young girls have been taught to block the descending flow of their menstruating wombs with tampons and commercial pads, to numb out any pain with chemicals, to practice a "feminine hygiene" that is fear of the wild feminine essence dressed up as cleanliness, with our power and intuition sanitized too.

Rebirth of the Temple of the Yoni

Yet the collective temple of our yoni is once again awakening to her glory. With this remembrance our ancient self-care rituals are rebirthing too.

Yoni steaming or vaginal steaming, as it is also known, is returning to mass consciousness—with popular magazine articles now featuring its benefits.

This feminine healing art has been traditionally practiced in many ancient cultures, including Mayan, African, Egyptian, Korean, to name but a few. By using hot water infused with healing herbs to gently steam open the yoni and root and penetrate the womb, physical, emotional, and energetic toxins can release. The practice is now becoming widespread across the world.

For me, the return of the feminine healing arts is a beautifully mysterious process. While there is an understandable desire to emphasize the medical benefits of these practices—which are said to include helping to heal infertility, cysts, fibroids, endometriosis—I sense the deepest medicine is for the feminine soul.

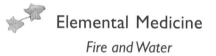 ## Elemental Medicine
Fire and Water

In feminine shamanic traditions the balancing power of fire and water is well known. Yoni steaming brings the blessing of water to cleanse, open, soften; to gently nurture our most intimate self with the mystery of the living waters.

The practice of the yoni smudge is less well known, yet also a very ancient tradition, harnessing the power of fire to cleanse, renew, and revitalize with healing smoke, bringing its orgasmic, enlivening gifts of the ascending energy to the yoni.

Originally the yoni smudge and the yoni steam also cycled with the energetic signatures of the dark moon and the full moon, weaving them together.

Like the yoni steam, the yoni smudge is recorded as a powerful ancient feminine healing art. Archaeologists have discovered papyrus in Egypt that record prescriptions given to women to sit over smoking resins of frankincense, allowing the smoke to enter their wombs to enhance their fertility.

These ancient papyri contain a wisdom that is also encoded in our feminine DNA and the ancestral and intuitive wisdom of our wombs—if we listen to this voice within.

Celtic Womb Priestesses
Reclaiming Our Yoni Rituals

Coming from a Celtic ancestry, I have had to search the akashic records in the dream time to remember these feminine healing rituals, as any written records of these healing arts being used in Britain were either lost or destroyed during the witch hunts. These hunts targeted wise women who practiced herbalism, midwifery, and the feminine healing arts—the source of wisdom for womb self-care rituals.

In 2013, on the eve of a Womb awakening retreat held in a Celtic round-house in the mystical heartlands of Cornwall, the Lyonesse of old legends, something magical happened—a coven of beautiful Womb priestesses visited me in the dream time to share their wisdom thread of the feminine healing arts.

The land we were staying on was very sacred and had been in use for at least five thousand years. Pottery remains found on the site depicted symbols of red downward-facing triangles—the ancient symbol of the sacred Womb. Clearly this was a place sacred to the Womb mysteries and the ancestral Womb shamans.

The vision that came to me in the dream time was shimmering with color and vibrancy, rich with the beauty of the feminine ways. A coven of Womb priestesses were swirling and spiraling in a mystical dance very similar to Sufi whirling, wearing gorgeous rainbow-colored skirts vivid with intricate patterns. Their movements were almost in slow motion, and the fluid beauty of their rainbow skirts, moving in a synchronized serpentine flow, was breathtaking.

Finally, their swirling dance stopped, and one by one each priestess came to a standstill, creating a geometric formation, with the expanse of each of their rainbow skirts extending to the floor, creating a beautiful, conical tent-like effect.

Now the rich scent of incense and healing resins began to arise, and I could feel and see that each woman was standing over a smudge bowl and that the expanse of their skirts was creating a womb-like enclosure for the smoke.

The priestesses communicated to me that this was an important feminine healing art they had used to cleanse and enliven the womb and yoni, both for healing and prophecy. They were wishing to transmit this wisdom again.

I had heard that the priestesses of Delphi, the famous Womb oracles, had crouched over a natural hole in the earth, receiving hot steam into their yoni, in order to prophesy, but I had not imagined it was a widespread practice.

Yet here were Celtic Womb priestesses who had sought contact with me in the dream time to let me know this was a practice that could be embraced by all women. It made perfect sense. The power of ritual smudging is widespread in most shamanic cultures, and it made womb-sense that it was a feminine healing art that could empower women to heal and restore the power of their wombs.

Yoni Steaming—Make Your Home a Temple of the Feminine Arts

Yoni steaming at home is a very simple process that takes about an hour. It is also a powerful time for prayer, contemplation, meditation, or devotional chanting and toning. You will need a bowl of hot water, fresh or dried herbs (not essential oils), and ideally a specially made yoni steam chair (although you can place the bowl in the toilet). Popular herbs used include motherwort, holy basil, chamomile, thyme, rose, mugwort, and red clover.

- ☽ Simmer the herbs in a pan of water for ten minutes.

- ☽ Allow to steep for at least five minutes.

- ☽ Pour the herbs and warm water into your yoni root steam bowl.

- ☽ Make sure the temperature is just right and not too hot!

- ☽ Sit on your chair over the bowl for ten minutes while the steam rises.

If you are not familiar with the practice or have health issues, it is advised that you contact a womb healer or seek guidance before you try the practice on your own. This is not to be practiced if you are pregnant or on the second half of your cycle if you are trying to conceive.

These feminine healing arts are powerful and simple. They invite us to create sacred space in the midst of our modern lives and include our womb in our self-care. Not only can they heal our physical womb, they can also heal our feminine soul by reconnecting us to the mystical beauty of our lost feminine traditions.

The wisdom is within you, and the power to heal is also within you. By nurturing and tending to your sacred fire within, something new can be born in your life.

THIRTY

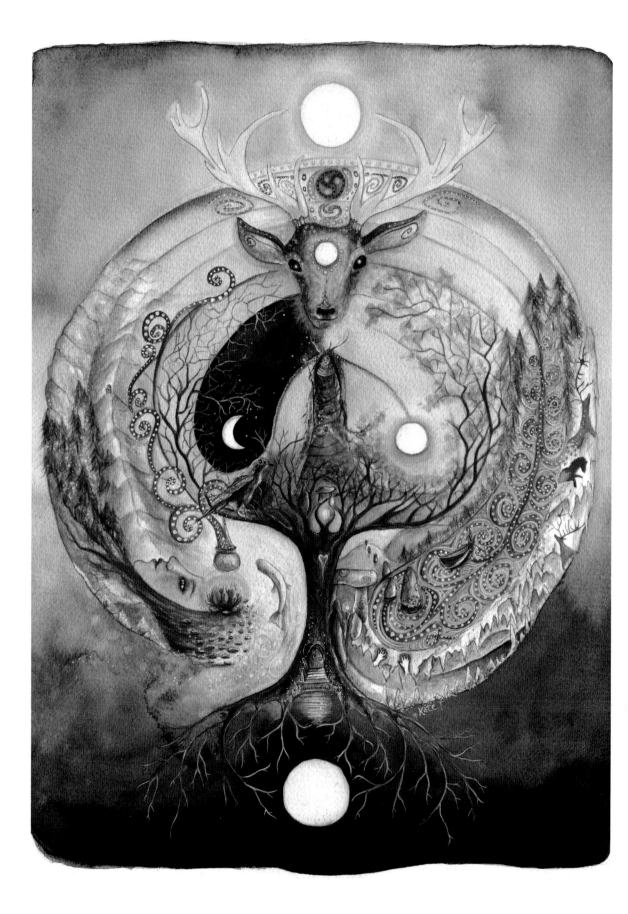

FEMININE ARCHETYPES

The Witch and the Priestess

I was asked about the iconic feminine archetypes of witch and priestess and the way these energies express within each of us and how we can interpret their soul medicine.

My sense is that every woman has a different relationship with these archetypes. For me, the witch represents the dark moon, the wise crone, the epiphany of wisdom, like Baba Yaga. I also feel her deeply connected to Earth, to the cycles, to the mystery of the dark-light-rebirth. I can feel how her power has been so acutely suppressed in this world. It is a power that does not and cannot serve patriarchy. It is pure primordial Womb power, and it has been demonized and an attempt has been made to destroy it—even trying to burn it at the stake. But it is eternal and cannot be destroyed and will always return from the deepest, wildest, fiercest roots.

In Irish tradition there is the Cailleach, who is the spirit of the land and brings us the witchy magic of connecting to the primordial essence of the earth elements, billions of years old, that are nonhuman. Then there is the banshee, faerie woman, who mediates with the human world. For me, she is a bridge to the supernatural ancestral roots of the wisdom of the priestess archetype.

The priestess is an emissary of the full moon and also the menstrual red river of the red moon. She is an aspect of the Magdalene, the *dakini,* the bridge weaver between worlds and the union weaver between the masculine and feminine and our wounded and whole selves. Whereas the witch lives in our deep, dark, inner forest, the priestess has entered the Temple of Resurrection to birth the light, to share her arts, to open to the medicine of sacred beauty. Her sexuality is a eucharist of the Divine Mother, bathing the world in an enchanted bliss of sensual enlightenment.

The witch is our fierce, uncompromising wisdom and power, a feminine power that has been banished and forbidden. We invoke this energy for revelation to awaken us into truth.

The priestess is the heart of our shakti, who builds the bridges between the duality of separation to bring healing, union, and the gifts of love and beauty. She raptures us back into the remembrance of the Womb's soft light of love.

Together they birth the witch-priestess: soft power, fierce beauty, wild truth.

 *Feminine Lunar Archetypes*

Which cyclical feminine archetype is calling to you? Tune into these two lists—which one do you feel attracted to the most *right now*?

Full Moon—The Inner Priestess

- ☽ Relational and sexual healing
- ☽ Working with scents and oils
- ☽ Dance, movement, music, sound

Dark Moon—The Inner Witch

- ☽ Nature magic and elemental power
- ☽ Shadow work and underworld magic
- ☽ Healing with herbs and essences

Dreaming Our Magic

THIRTY-ONE

WOMB OF THE WORLD

Circle of the Ancestors

In the heart of Miami lives an ancient time portal into the land of the ancestors.

On the Virgo full moon of 2017, we stepped through a magical portal back in time to the land of the Mayaimi aboriginal peoples of southeastern Florida. This dimensional entryway to the Womb of the world is encircled by the consciousness of the dolphins and the sea creatures that once swam within the dream time of the human heart.

The night before our pilgrimage, a perfectly round full moon hung over the Miami skyline—a city reaching up for the stars, while forgetting its roots within the fertile wet earth. Fast cars, condos, and streetlights, created over the past fifty years, are watched over by the ancient moon mother, almost five billion years old, who has seen many human-made civilizations rise and fall under the cosmic gaze of her light.

As we drove through the middle of crazy downtown Miami, it seemed so unlikely that we were approaching a sacred indigenous site. We knew we had to open ourselves to the hidden dimension of consciousness beneath the superficial layer of human-made creations.

Our destination was the Mayaimi Stone Circle (the Miami Circle at Brickell Point), a prehistoric ceremonial circle discovered in 1998 under a building demolition in the heart of the city. Some legends say its discovery was an apocalypse switch, a portal ushering in a new cycle on Earth.

The Jewel Blue Gateway

The Mayaimi Circle stands at the mouth of the Miami River, bizarrely but perfectly snuggled in between towering downtown skyscrapers, where it meets the protected jewel blue waters of the Bay of Biscayne on its way into the great Atlantic Ocean.

It is a perfect thirty-eight-foot-wide ceremonial circle, carved into the Florida limestone bedrock at least two thousand years ago (some archaeologists say ten thousand years ago) by a people out of time, living in a water world, dreaming. The circle is lined by twenty-four carved basins, which some researchers believe are shaped as the totem animals of the region—shark, dolphin, turtle, crocodile, whale, manatee, and others. Found buried within the ceremonial circle was the full skeleton of a shark marking the east-west axis of the site, a complete sea turtle shell, and a dolphin skull, as well as finely crafted ceremonial black basalt axes that originated six hundred miles away.

In addition to the twenty-four larger basins, hundreds of smaller post holes were carved into the rock. Some archaeologists speculate these were used as a type of astronomical calendar, anchor standing stones, or other posts that marked celestial events, analogous to Stonehenge of Britain.

When we arrived at the circle, we first went to the water's edge to pay our respects to the Great Mother. We then opened our hearts and began to tune into the unseen dimension of reality that the first peoples called the Real World, the hidden world of energy behind surface forms. Immediately, we were greeted by guardians of the site, archaic humans with broad faces and ceremonial paint who appeared more like Neanderthals than modern humans. A man let us know how to honor and open the site, singing in the spirits of the human and animal ancestors, circling in the direction of the sun, giving offerings at the eastern point of sunrise and the western point of sunset and finally the south and north. An old woman then appeared who looked us in the eyes to silently transmit deeper layers of energy and information.

She said, "Earth is menstruating again; her fertility will be reborn."

Dolphins, Dragons, and World Navels

For thousands of years, this ceremonial circle has been the spirit keeper of the southeastern tip of North America. It is a world navel or direct portal into the Womb of the world and acts as a gateway or bridge of consciousness between the land peoples and the sea creatures, between the salt and sweet waters, and between Earth and other dimensions. It is also connected to world navel sites across the globe, whose threads hold the world together in a dreaming web of Gaia's consciousness.

The site is located at a meeting of the great waters and at a very activated node within Earth's dragon grids, which served to amplify the power of shamanic interdimensional and interspecies communication and co-creativity. It was a spiritual telecommunication center where shamanic calls could be placed to whales, dolphins, sea turtles, and other animal ancestors, who worked together with the humans to sing life into being. The Mayaimi point is also home to an ancient water dragon, one of the primordial mothers of creation whose subterranean stirrings can cause great upheavals at times and who is directly linked to the creation and destruction of Atlantis.

Despite the march of time and all the changes of the modern world, the earth magic at this site is as potent as ever. We need only glide our fingertips across the veils to touch the soul of the world as she patiently awaits our invitation to flood her consciousness back into our lives like the incoming tide.

The Legacy of Big Water

The history of this aboriginal circle is as beautiful as it is devastating. For thousands of years, the first peoples of the Americas lived relatively unchanged in this enchanted land of Mayaimi, or "Big Water," the namesake of the now massive city of Miami with its six million inhabitants and unearthly cityscape and beach parties. Only a hundred years ago, fewer than five hundred people lived in this sacred water world wilderness.

Like the Mississippian cultures, the south Florida indigenous peoples sculpted the land into a living ceremonial landscape of sacred earthworks, mounds, embankments, pyramids, canals, and pools, often taking the form of sacred womb circles but also in the shape of humans, animals, or dream figures. Crescent-shaped moon pools reflected the soft nighttime glow of moonlight and the Milky Way and were likely used in lustral bathing rituals similar to those found throughout the ancient world. The power of lunar-ray-infused waters mirrored the Divine Womb.

From the beginning of time, earth peoples lived in harmony with this land until the coming of the Europeans and the ensuing cultural and ecological devastation that followed. The last members of the Tequesta tribe who lived here were driven off the land in the late 1700s—many killed and sold into slavery, with a small band fleeing to safety in Cuba. Villages burned, families were destroyed, the old ways forgotten.

When the indigenous peoples left, the Mayaimi Circle ceremonial site was nearly lost, lying hidden and buried beneath several feet of soil. But in 1998 it was rediscovered during a routine archaeological survey for the building of a luxury high-rise condominium complex, which attracted nationwide attention. A massive legal battle began to preserve the site, and thanks to the heroics of many earth protectors within both the government and the general public, the state of Florida eventually bought the land to put it under preservation where it can be visited today.

Mayan Civilization in the Americas

We percolated on the power of this site and its resonance with the Yucatan and asked if the Mayaimi Circle was of Mayan origin. The circle is architecturally unique, being the only structure carved directly into bedrock on the entire East Coast of America, and in many ways it is more reminiscent of the stone-working technologies of the Maya, or perhaps an even older culture of the descendants of Atlantis.

Is it a coincidence that the name Mayaimi is so close to that of the Maya, who lived in the region of Mayam, the indigenous civilization located just three hundred miles away, across the Gulf of Mexico, at the time that the

Mayaimi Circle was being built? Despite overwhelming evidence to the contrary, many mainstream archaeologists still mistakenly believe that indigenous cultures such as these could not have had contact with each other because they did not possess the sea-faring skills to navigate across large bodies of water.

The Yucatan Maya were the most powerful and influential culture of the region exactly because they were accomplished mariners and traders, their trade routes spanning the width and breadth of Mesoamerica and the Gulf of Mexico. Jade artifacts from the Guatemala Maya have been found as far as the island of Antigua, 1,700 miles away. Maize, the staple crop of the Maya, was first found in North America among the Mayaimi and related tribes of Southeast Florida. How did it arrive? It had to have been brought across by Mayan traders.

As researcher Gary Daniels notes in his article on the subject, one Mayan group was the Itza Maya, and several towns in Florida and Georgia are called Itsate or Itzate, meaning the "Itza Place." Another town in Florida is Uquetan, a variant spelling of Yucatan. One of the only five-sided Native American sacred mounds outside Mayan lands is found at the Etowah Mounds archaeological site of Georgia, just north of Florida. And this is just the tip of a very big iceberg of Mayan cultural influence still found in the southeastern tip of North America.

 ## Sacred Place of Water

Another link between the Maya and the Mayaimi lies in their profound reverence for the waters of life, the freshwater springs and rivers that sustain life on Earth. Some of the most important sacred sites of the Yucatec Maya, including the pyramid complex of Chichen Itza, were built on top of cenotes—sacred freshwater caverns and rivers extending deep into the earth, the original temples and places of worship. And just as the name Mayaimi means "Big Water," so did the Mayan word *Lakamha,* the original name given to the famous temple city of Palenque, mean "Big Water."

Southeastern Florida is truly a water world. Stunning turquoise oceans surround the peninsula on all sides. But this is only one part of the story: underneath the entire state, as well as parts of Georgia, South Carolina, and Alabama, is the Floridan aquifer system, one of the most important freshwater aquifer systems in the world. This hidden waterworld is more than one hundred thousand square miles in size and in places extends down into the earth to a depth of more than three thousand feet, with vast underground lakes, caverns, and rivers hidden to the eyes of its surface dwellers.

Few modern inhabitants of Florida realize that the seemingly solid limestone ground under their feet is just a thin roof overlying one of the greatest underwater cave systems on Earth, buoyed up by the hidden waters flowing beneath.

More than any other region of the United States, Florida is gifted with an abundance of mineral-rich and crystal-clear freshwater springs and pools that bubble up to the surface from this immense subterranean aquifer, opening like mysterious passageways that lead down into the center of Earth, where, unseen, they all interconnect in a vast network of underground rivers and pools. They are truly the veins and arteries of Earth, the sacred Womb waters of Gaia, and the lifeblood of the plants and animals who depend upon them for their survival.

Some of these underwater caves and rivers underneath Florida have been explored by divers down to depths of hundreds of feet, but we have only glimpsed the smallest fraction of this magical underworld, and many explorers, fascinated by the blue abyss of these water portals, have been lost as they tried to go too deep.

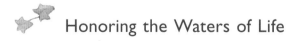 ## Honoring the Waters of Life

To the indigenous peoples of Florida, the Mayaimi Circle was a guardian temple of the sacred waterways, honoring them as the fountain of life, the liquid feminine essence of Earth, which allowed humans and animals to live on her surface—and without which we could not survive. To pollute or disrespect them was a threat to life itself.

This sacred portal offers us an invitation to harmonize ourselves with the resonance of ancient Earth and her peoples, to honor the water of life, so we can remember who we truly are and what is being asked of us in this time of great change.

During our time in Miami (Big Water), we had been intuitively feeling other nodes on the worldwide Womb web, other water chakras, such as Hawaii and Australia.

A friend had also given us a film to watch, *Whaledreamers,* a documentary about the remembrance and revival of the ancient tradition of communicating with the spirit of the sea creatures, as practiced by tribes such as the original peoples of Australia.

On our last night, at a restaurant overlooking the swaying waters of the harbor, the waiter found us before we left to say he felt called to show us a video on his iPhone. It was footage of him swimming with a wild pod of dolphins in Hawaii. It felt like the dolphins had heard our prayers through the songlines of the sea.

Water is the creator of life, and a memory keeper and wisdom transmitter. When we listen to her ebb and flow, the secrets of the world sing out to us.

Resources

Daniels, Gary. "Were the Maya Mining Gold in Georgia?" December 26, 2011. LostWorlds.org.

THIRTY-TWO

Dakini Magic

Jewel in the Lotus Womb

In 1996, at the age of twenty-four, I was called to the mystical lands of the Himalayas of Northern India to play, explore, and immerse in a new magical world of spirituality, where I would remember the womb-song of our inner dakini DNA.

Over twenty years later, this seed of cultural exploration eventually led me to the hidden pearl of sacred feminine shakti worship and to learn of a lost world of Tibetan Khandros, female shamans, and the wisdom of their pre-Vedic and pre-Buddhist traditions.

As I set out into the foothills of the ancient Himalayas, I was fascinated by the bright, magical world that was unfolding before me. I read *The Tibetan Book of Living and Dying* as I sipped chai and pondered over other scriptures that were a world away from what I'd heard back home in church. This was an alternate universe with dakinis, divine mothers, and dragonesses.

One evening a Tibetan monk invited me and my friends to take a yoga class with him in the morning. At sunrise. I am a child of the moon, a midnight soul—mornings do not suit me! A lighthearted bet was made by my friends and the monk that there was no way, ever, that I would go. I had never done yoga before and was not in any way drawn to try it out.

I had little intention of going unless the sun himself decided to shake me out of bed. Yet just before the sun rose, as if the "bet" were a mystical alarm

clock, arise I did. So I experienced my first ever yoga class on a rooftop watching the sunrise over the white-tipped Himalayas and marveling with childlike delight that I could touch my toes.

I had dipped my now-touched toes in the path of the yogini, which was singing out to me from my very bones, despite my resistance and sense of mischief.

Next, I went to a mass blessing ceremony with His Holiness the Dalai Lama at the temple in Dharamshala, in the Himalayas of Northern India, where the Tibetan government-in-exile is based. After standing in line for hours, I finally turned a corner, walking in slow procession, toward the Dalai Lama. I "felt" him before I saw him. Face-to-face, staring into his deep-brown eyes, I received his blessing as he placed a ceremonial scarf round my neck. In return, I offered him a ceremonial scarf called a *khata,* to honor him and offer my respect.

A khata is a traditional ceremonial scarf made of silk used in Tibet and Mongolia that symbolizes purity, goodwill, auspiciousness, compassion, and the pure heart of the giver. The tangible sense of occult power flowing through this exchange stayed with me for hours, creating trembling sensations throughout my whole body.

During this time, I had the gift of also attending an early morning *puja,* or prayer, where we joined the throngs of Tibetan people walking through the narrow streets at 4 a.m. It was an incredibly magical sight to see many ancient-looking Tibetan women dressed in their traditional attire singing *om-mani-padme-hum* as they spiraled their prayer wheels, and we all descended down the dark narrow hill toward the Dalai Lama Temple.

At the temple we gathered inside for a long puja ceremony, permeated with the sounds of the Tibetan chanting. After the puja, nearby smiling old Tibetan nuns passed me the yak butter tea that is served as part of the ritual, which I forced down with polite smiles. I'm pretty sure the nuns knew how bad it tasted to me, and this was the source of their hilarity! Afterward, we moved outside and listened to the Dalai Lama speak. As the sun rose, flooding us with rays of soft light, an old Tibetan woman wrapped honorific prayer scarves round an ancient-looking tree, sobbing her heart out at his words, and I found myself weeping with her.

Hearing the Feminine Soul Songs of Tibet

Later, in 2004, I once again reconnected with this lineage, meeting my Tibetan soul sister, whose family and lineage came from the nomadic tribes of the high plains of Tibet. Through this I became imbued with the magic of the more nomadic and shamanistic elements of Tibetan Buddhism that exist under the current monastic religion.

One time, in a private home of a community of Tibetans-in-exile, we gathered together at 4 a.m. on the morning of Losar, the traditional Tibetan New Year. Sitting in darkness, with just a few lit candles flickering, we nibbled on traditional Tibetan food prepared for this auspicious day.

In this liminal atmosphere, a young woman sat with us who had just made the arduous three-month trek across the Himalayan mountains to escape from Tibet, which has been occupied by China since 1949, killing or oppressing many Tibetans. In the darkness, she began to sing a series of haunting, otherworldly traditional nomadic songs, which were originally sung as spirit songs to the land and animals, often by women. I was told she was a renowned singer back in her homeland.

As the sun rose, we all traveled together to the Dalai Lama Temple for the more traditional celebrations, circumambulating the temple and spinning the prayer wheels.

Yet those nomadic songs were still vibrating through my soul, calling me to a place deep within—a hidden feminine space of ancient magic, where words could not reach.

Gateway of Enlightenment

Since the advent of patriarchy, as it manifests in many traditions—from Christian to Buddhist—the embodied feminine wisdom of the female shaman has disappeared from the sunlit worlds of state ceremonies, temples, and scriptures.

Yet her wisdom still sings on, in the sacred body of Earth and woman.

In Sanskrit the word *dakini* means "sky dancer," and the Tibetan equivalent is *khandro,* meaning a female tantric priestess who travels shamanically through the multidimensional space of the cosmic Womb, the Womb of Earth, and the inner womb. Like many shamans, one aspect of the work of the dakini-priestess was to carry the souls of the dead back to the celestial Womb, to the quantum home of the Divine Mother, or to assist new souls birthing into this realm.

Another sacred role was to take initiates into a cosmic-psychic death-and-rebirth journey, traveling along the same mystical pathways, while still alive. Dakinis were known as playful, mysterious, mischievous initiators—sexually enlightened shamanesses who flowed on the nondual rivers of shakti and could easily live in many worlds.

The secret of their power was the illuminated black hole within their wombs.

Dakinis were famous for a mysterious twilight language, similar to the language of the birds of the Celtic priestesses, which was a song vibration of the feminine cosmic soul. In her book *Traveller in Space,* June Campbell attempts to unravel the lunar pathways of the feminine mysticism at the heart of Tibetan Buddhism, which deeply infuse this tradition.

She says of the twilight language of the dakinis: "Essentially, the notion was of symbolic language, whose musical sounds could . . . be heard mystically by advanced meditators. Texts were often said to have been received by the Lama through a whispered communication by the divine voices of the dakinis."

This connects to the tradition of *terma,* or treasure texts, in Tibetan Buddhism. These mystical texts are conveyed symbolically and are also embedded in the cosmic consciousness or the dragon body of the earth goddess or the mitochondrial DNA of the female, which can be accessed at a later time, when humanity is ready to hear the soul of the universal womb singing out her wisdom to them. The ultimate treasure texts lives within the dharma womb of the awakened yogini, such as Tibetan priestess Yeshe Tsogyal, and in the pregnant potentiality of every woman.

Campbell goes on to say: "Standing outside the boundaries of language as we know it, the Dakini 'twilight language' was a metaphor for divine transcendence, a state of 'otherness' that was transmitted through the body of the female dakini, and . . . the female voice of the Dakini."

Tsultrim Allione, author of *Women of Wisdom,* discusses "The Song of the Vajra," poetic tantric chants of awakening said to be in the language of the dakinis. She describes how these feminine sounds "vibrate in the body . . . and bring forth waves which massage the vibration of the being, bringing an integration with the spherical sounds of the universe."

Songs of Enlightenment, Voice of the Womb

I still remember the mystery of that magical Losar morning, and my cells still vibrate with that spherical cosmic song of the mysterious feminine, coming forth from a woman who had lost everything, except her voice and her precious inner song.

Her voice poured itself out into the darkened night of new beginnings, as a lament, as a prayer, as a celebration, as a remembrance, as a cry of the lost feminine soul, still in union with Earth. It spoke directly to the heart of my feminine self. It told me, as if speaking directly from the dakini DNA: "This voice is within you. Wake up."

Om mani padme hum—Honor the jewel in the lotus womb

Resources

Allione, Tsultrim. *Women of Wisdom*. Ithaca, N.Y.: Snow Lion, 2000.
Campbell, June. *Traveller in Space*. London and New York: Continuum, 2002.

THIRTY-THREE

GODDESS INITIATION

The Power of Kali

The kali energy comes in many different forms. The goddess Kali is dark matter, the Dark Mother's primordial creative flow, and also the divine mirror. She mirrors back what is within us, and our deepest soul. She removes all obstacles to what we truly desire. If there is a lot of fear and resistance and inner desires that are in complete opposition to the external life we are living, this energy can be experienced as frightening, cathartic, or intense. Yet when we flow deeper on her dark rivers, the kali energy becomes something so deliciously dark and deep, so profoundly soft, like black velvet, which brings an incredible tenderness and openness in this womb of dissolution. This letting go is really an invitation to birth something new.

> *Tandava is the dance of creation and of dissolution. It is the dance in which Shakti will vanquish Shiva, reestablishing the power of the feminine, imposing her rhythm and inviting us in our turn to create and destroy in an infinite cycle. Kali, through the tandava, expresses the creativity of chaos.*
>
> DANIEL ODIER, *TANTRIC KALI*

This quote reminded me of one the oracular visions shared in *Womb Awakening*: "Could I open my womb eye to see the truth of the shadow side of my wild sexuality to reclaim my power? When I went down into my womb eye to see the truth, I saw a glowing red ruby jewel pulsing and vibrating. The jewel exploded into a red dragon woman who started dancing wildly and seductively with the trickster in his black top hat, long coat tails, and walking stick. Suddenly, the red dragon woman turned into Kali who danced more wildly and fiercely. She took the trickster's walking stick and passionately pinned him to the ground. He turned into Shiva, the divine trickster, who took Kali's shakti. In her wild abandon, Kali stood on his chest, her foot on his heart; he was feeding off her shakti. She cut off the supply and took her shakti back: Black One, Creation before Light, Beyond Time."

It also reminded me of a time when I danced with the energy of Kali . . .

While I was living in a remote village in India, studying Indian temple dance with other women, we learned that a famous guru and devotee of Shiva was coming to a nearby town. There would be ten thousand people gathering to see him. He had heard about us Western girls dancing Odissi, an ancient Indian classical dance, and invited us to perform at his mass *satsang*. Our dance teacher was frantic and decided we had to perform a *tandava* dance for the guru, which meant we had one week to learn this difficult new dance that was beyond my capacity.

Suddenly, our beautiful village routine of dance, prayers, rest, and eating, which undulated in waves every day, was disrupted. I was not a professional dancer and didn't want to perform at the satsang; it felt so pressurized. I tried to wriggle out of it, but the dance teacher wouldn't let me. Instead, every morning after my devotional singing to Kali with the Brahmin, I sat alone and prayed hard to Kali for an intervention. A day before the performance, we learned that the guru had unexpectedly been taken sick and had to cancel all his tour dates! I was convinced Kali had had her way (and felt a little guilty about it too). I felt how the rhythm of the feminine had been restored. How Kali cuts through the overly solar world of perfection and hard work, where we push ourselves to perform for outside sources. She invites us inside. Back to black.

For me, this was a vital lesson into the nature of sacred dance—it wasn't about external performance or pressures, it was a sacred art of internal connectivity and private devotion.

The feminine arts are very much about aligning with the natural rhythms of feminine energy; the cycles of the moon, the daily circle of the sun, and the seasonal cycles of sun, rain, and rebirth. When we dance or sing and make our offerings from within this sacred circle of experience, we are rooted into the primordial energy of vitality that grows and falls in cycles and animates life.

In the village, I was invited into the beauty of daily rituals that honor these cycles. On Tuesdays the women of the village would leave a vivid crimson hibiscus flower for Durga outside their front door, along with a stick of lit incense. I would walk along the dusty road, illuminated by these earthy scarlet offerings, soaked in the blessings of the goddess. Along the way, I would also handpick colorful flowers from the abundance of nature, to leave as offerings to the deities when I arrived at our simple dance studio. Lighting the incense, adorning the statues with freshly picked flowers, and then chanting and making the offering of a dance prayer initiated each day.

I felt the power of this daily, domestic devotion so deeply. It created everyday enchantment. This was the power of feminine magic; rooted in the ebbs and flows of everyday life.

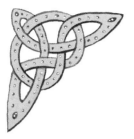

THIRTY-FOUR

LADY SATURN

Lineage of the Cosmic Witch

A once-in-a-lifetime grand conjunction unfolded on the 2020 solstice: Lady Saturn, the dark goddess of initiation and restriction, embraced Lord Jupiter, the optimistic god of abundance and expansion, in a frisson of union. The witch of the dark woods with all her wild wisdom did the fox-trot with Pan, the virile god of growth, in the sacred groves of worship to give birth to something entirely new that brings a restored way of balance.

In Egyptian tradition, this celestial union was also revered. The deity Osiris was equated with Saturn (Lord of the Underworld) and the Goddess Isis was associated with Jupiter, the planet of good fortune and resurrection. Both the gods and planets have a feminine/masculine aspect, one descending and one rising. When they unite into alchemical union a portal of rebirth is created.

From my sense, on this conjunction Lady Saturn showed her dark feminine face, the Void.

As astrologers reported across the world: "On the night of December 21, 2020, the winter solstice, Jupiter and Saturn will appear so closely aligned in our sky that they will look like a double planet. This close approach is called a conjunction."

Ancient people understood that astrology was a cosmic guiding force not only in our personal lives but in the great collective cycles of our cultures and societies.

Wise men and women of the past studied these unusual cosmic events, knowing that civilizations were created and destroyed on big astrological waves.

The 2020 grand conjunction of these two major planets creates a Christmas star—not unlike the one said to have heralded the birth of Christ two thousand years ago.

According to Sheffield astronomer Professor David W. Hughes, author of *The Star of Bethlehem Mystery,* the stellar event that announced the birth of Christ happened in 7 BCE and . . . drum roll . . . was created by an astounding conjunction of the planets Saturn and Jupiter, creating a "star" visible in the sky—just like the 2020 grand conjunction. Except that, as prophesized, this second coming is in Aquarius.

Astrologer and author Jessica Adams says, "The Magi, the three wise men, gave very specific astrological meaning to the Jupiter-Saturn conjunction. This was rare. A triple conjunction. An unusual alignment." These Saturn-Jupiter alignments are portents of change: "As far back as the 15th century, it was thought that these celestial meetings between Jupiter and Saturn chimed with important historical events. The rise and fall of empires, the birth of religions."

Hughes observes in an article that "the Star of Bethlehem was probably a triple conjunction of Saturn and Jupiter in the constellation of Pisces, the significance of which was only obvious to the Magi of Babylonia. This occurred in 7 BC and events indicate that Jesus Christ was probably born in the Autumn of that year, around October, 7 BC."

Winter solstice has always been a portal beloved by Lady Saturn. The old festival of Saturnalia—in honor of Saturn—was held between December 17 and 23, over the solstice period. It was surrounded by feasting, celebration, and the disruption of normal hierarchies. By Roman times this festival was visioned as being for a male god, a god of the Underworld like Osiris, but originally Saturn was a dark goddess. A Womb goddess. A rebirther. Her womb was seen as a dark, restrictive netherworld container whose primal mystery birthed the light.

On a personal level I have been journeying with Lady Saturn for quite a while.

In fact, it was my Saturn return many moons ago at age twenty-eight that hit me like a hard, black stiletto and led me onto the path of feminine wisdom, personal healing, and womb awakening. I then deepened my acquaintance with Saturn at the start of 2018. This astrological archetype presides over all our grand transformations and waits for us patiently with her dark womb wisdom.

This time, Saturn appeared in a dream the night before an abdominal surgery to remove a large fibroid from my womb so I would be able to conceive. I had asked spirit for a dream. I thought I needed something inspiring, illuminating, and maybe a bit spiritually fancy. Instead, the queen of the Underworld greeted me with a smirk and led me down into her realm in the Earth Womb.

She was sexy, magnificent, darkly humorous, vast, tricksy, astounding; she was the purity of life force throbbing at the heart of creation with a wildly purring power.

She is the darkness that birthed light. She was fertility and feminine magic embodied.

In exchange for a baby, my heart's desire, I had to let go of everything, she told me. It was like a fairy tale, and I was walking with the cosmic witch of the dark woods, who was picking me apart, bone by bone, boiling me up in her great cauldron stew.

How much did I want it? she asked me. And what was I prepared to let go of to bring through a new birth that I had been dreaming on for so many years?

When I woke up, I remembered an old picture of Mae West, wearing a shiny, tight black dress and bat wings (looking like an underworld angel), which became a guiding image. When everyone else was looking up to the light, I was down in the dark, rummaging through the rubble of my life, letting go of everything so I could keep my side of the bargain. It made sense. A fibroid is something that doesn't belong in our wombs and prevents us conceiving and birthing our desires. It's something that needs to be removed so that fertility can be restored.

I sense these times have a similar flavor. Lady Saturn is asking us to let go of what is no longer working and restore our fertility so that we can conceive something new. She is asking us to listen to that new tune, a new birth, pulsing in the rich and fertile blackness of the earth womb.

Lady Saturn is the darkness of wisdom, of Sophia. She is the grand cosmic witch.

Saturn brings us a fullness of knowing, a spherical wisdom that encompasses many nuances, not just a one-sided "goodness" taught to us by the cultural wasteland. Like the famous quote by Mae West, she teases us with paradox, quipping: *When I'm good, I'm very good, but when I'm bad I'm better.* She is deconstructing the man-made prison of the "good girl," made to keep us small, tamed, and controlled. She teaches us that life is many things: wild, primal, raw, cyclical, regenerative, pristine, majestic, but never safe. Lady Saturn comes bearing primal wisdom.

Our cosmic ecology is complex, beyond the thinking mind and its straightforward rules. *We have to think from inside the nature that we are. We have to learn to see with the eyes of Sophia.* When she is dark, she is wet and fertile and full of growth; when she rises and ascends, it is with a sumptuous, joyful, spontaneous flowering.

We all have this wild, primal knowing inside us; this is our inner *witchblood*—our nous, our womb knowing, our gut instinct, our intuition that *tells us the truth.*

A new way is already forming, as our body wisdom leads the way and our souls sing out. Look carefully and you will see the tendrils of new growth all around you. Life is speaking clearly, simply, loudly, in many different ways, guiding you.

This gives us an astounding yet complex and challenging opportunity to begin again, and we know in our deep heart wombs that the old world wasn't working.

Enter Lady Saturn and Lord Jupiter to wise us up *and* give us the faith in the future. This is *birth work*; it requires depth, diligence, and love to create anew.

The Dark Lady is a tough mistress because birth is tough primal work; it can feel like it is splitting us in two, which in some ways it is, as a new creation emerges. It can also feel ecstatic, joyful, exhilarating, as our hearts reach out to love again.

We do not know what this astrological portal has initiated for our world, but we must enter with full heart, with full hope, with our wisdom switched on and our courage set on fire.

In this grand drama, we are all the midwife, the mother, and the birthing babe.

Resources

Adams, Jessica. "The Star of Bethlehem in Astrology" (blog). December 7, 2020. JessicaAdams.com.

———. "The Great Conjunction in Aquarius" (blog). Nov 30, 2020. JessicaAdams.com.

Hughes, David W. *The Star of Bethlehem Mystery.* London: Dent, 1979.

———. "The Star of Bethlehem." *Nature* 264 (1976): 512–17.

The Witch Ziroonderel
Collecting thunderbolts
among her Cabbages

THIRTY-FIVE

SCARLET WOMAN

Temple of the Feminine Arts

For many of us the *other* Mary is calling out to us. She is the face of the forbidden feminine and her sacred arts, who had a red veil drawn across her life.

Much as I appreciate Mary Magdalene's role as a preacher and teacher, as an apostle of the apostles, as depicted in the four extracanonical gospels—the Gospels of Mary, Thomas, and Philip and the Pistis Sophia—the Magdalene I know is so much more than that.

She is a wild, untamed feminine force that can never be captured or appropriated by any institution or belief system. She represents a lineage of magical women and feminine arts. Her eyes are magic doorways—bold and frank, confronting, daring. She is *too much* to handle, a boundary crosser, a rebel, a lover, a provocateur—a holy sexual wildfire that will not be extinguished until she has set the world alight. She is the lightbearer, the truthbringer, the one who loved so much she went *all* the way—and in doing so initiated the masculine into his power. She reminds us of the magical temple that lives inside the bodies of all women.

This Magdalene essence can express in many ways. One of the ways this wild Magdalene essence touched me as a teenager was through the pop icon Madonna.

As a young girl who had just passed through her menarche with no guidance and no female leadership, Madonna saucily twirled her conical bra at me as a feminist trailblazer. She taught me that you didn't have to be an actual virgin—you could be *like* a virgin. Your virginity could renew. She sang of a beloved who made her feel "touched for the very first time. With nothing to hide." It sounded like a holy union.

She was also bold, with big bad-ass ovaries, bitchy in all the best ways. She prayed ardently before every show—and then danced a circle round religion. Her stage show was a church of the feminine awakening. She was a female pope. She helped me understand that the feminine was not always sweet and quiet. The feminine was wild power.
There was an alchemical feminine: the Magdalene.

This alchemical feminine power is within us—and can never be owned or controlled. Its power is the vastness behind creation. It is the Womb of God.

Geisha
Scarlet Woman of the East

This archetype of the scarlet woman exists around the world, often veiled from sight. In Buddhism, it was female courtesan-prostitutes who funded Buddha's education to initiate him.

In the native feminine traditions of Japan, Michele Marra tells how "courtesans' songs became transformed into a Bodhisattva's offer of enlightenment, while their promises of physical intimacy were equated with offers of spiritual salvation." He shares how Buddhism "managed to appropriate much of the power believed to be possessed by shamanesses in the native Japanese tradition," which calls to mind that other sacred, yet taboo, woman of Japan—the geisha.

The origins of the Japanese geisha are lost in time, but it is easy to intuitively see that they belong to a long tradition of feminine temple arts, originally practiced ceremonially by priestesses and female shamans. Like the Indian *devadasi,* temple dancers who performed in sacred dance ritual and ceremony in Hindu temples, geishas are famed for the feminine arts—as sacred dancers, exquisite musicians, ceremonialists, soul soothers, and keepers of the sacred courtesan arts—and renowned for their beauty, wisdom, and grace.

Similarly, in Europe, after the feminine temples had fallen, obscuring the true roots of the feminine healing arts, the female priestesses and shamans were later demoted to be "just" singers, dancers, courtesans, and entertainers serving their male gods and priests, while their incredible abilities to shape-shift realities by opening artistic dimensional doorways into the feminine realm of creation were diminished and denied.

Yet in the striking red-and-white color signature of the geishas, the colors of shaman witches and the red and white moon cycle, their swirling vortex fan dances, and their tea ceremonies, pouring the fountain of life into the cup of blessings, we can feel their ancient Womb magic and hints of a feminine lineage.

Chinese poet and womb shaman Lao-tzu (c. 604–531 BCE) wrote these inspired word-doorways: "The feminine values are the fountain of bliss. Know the masculine, Keep to the feminine." The feminine has kept singing and dancing her doorways of creation open, and now the roots of these secrets are emerging to bloom again.

Resources

Lao Tzu quote from Ji, Liu Liang. *Ancient Chinese Wisdom: Thoughts of Bodhidharma, Lao Tzu, Confucius, Sun Tzu, Zhuang Zhou, Mencius, Han Fei and many more.* Self-published: CreateSpace, 2016.

Marra quote from "In This Issue." *The Journal of Asian Studies* 52, no. 1 (February 1993): 1–2. Marra's article "The Buddhist Mythmaking of Defilement: Sacred Courtesans in Medieval Japan" appears on pages 49–65 of this journal.

THIRTY-SIX

Priestess Path

Story of the Holy Whore

The Goddess is a mother, but she is also a lover. The love goddess, an aspect of the Great Goddess, connects us to the path of beauty and the delights of sacred sexuality and the healing power of pleasure. The love goddess is known by many names across different cultures, such as Venus, Ishtar, Inanna, Bast, Oshun, Xochiquetzal, Lalita, Rosalie, Freya, Aine, Branwen, and many others. Often a love goddess is associated with the moon, sexuality, fertility, and magic.

Pleasure, beauty, and fertility are not just physical or reproductive attributes but are also spiritual qualities and dimensions of feminine magic that anyone can embody. This energy is our innate awen, our anima, our shakti, our kundalini, our wild holy serpent power of life-force essence.

We can be fertile with creativity, or full of the beauty of compassion, or rich with Earth's simple pleasures. On the path of feminine magic, we court these powers to become a *courtesan of life*.

Over time, these goddesses have often had their feminine powers veiled or demoted, and their priestesses and magical orders have been forgotten or diminished as whores or prostitutes.

In Sumeria, now modern-day Iraq, the priestesses of the love goddess Inanna-Ishtar were famously demoted to become sacred prostitutes, and their epic skills of spiritual courtship, beauty, dance, art, shamanic feminine practice, and soul doula-ship were reduced to sexual currency.

Feminist scholar H. Meenee writes in "Sacred Prostitutes and Temple Slaves: The 'Sexual Priestesses' of Aphrodite" that hierodules were "young women dedicated to the Love Goddess in order to serve as her 'sexual priestesses.' They are more commonly known as sacred prostitutes."

As priestesses of the goddess, under female rulership, women's sacred body power was considered to be the earthly embodiment of the goddess she served—capable of conveying blessings and sacred sacraments. Her magical arts were revered as sacred threshold powers of birth, menstruation, death, resurrection, initiation, and rebirth. Her womb was the sovereign throne of her sexual magic, conveying a potent spiritual substance, an elixir and soma of immortality that was the source of her authority. As a spiritual leader, initiator, and healer, she held a place of respect and divine freedom.

When the goddess temples came under male authority and priesthoods and when male gods were also independently worshipped, the priestesses' sacred sexual powers were colonized and devoted to the male god; her music, her dance, her prayers, her sex power were dedicated to him. Her serpent allurements of awakened kundalini could stimulate his fertilizing power of communion with the earthly goddess woman. In this way, the priestess could be known as the wife, mistress, or concubine of the male god. In later times, she would consummate the sacred marriage with a temple priest or the king.

She was either celibate or celibate only during certain ritual times; she could be married or single. She was not a prostitute for any man, and it was once considered a terrible crime, akin to a curse, to defile a sacred priestess. There is little evidence sacred prostitution as reported by Herodotus ever existed, and if it did, then it was likely operated as a form of religiously sanctioned rape to disempower and humiliate women, as the feminine traditions were destroyed. These supposed customs represent an abuse of women's sexual power, not empowerment, and may have been the fate of indigenous priestesses who were overthrown from their seats of power and forced into a prostitution of their skills.

For many modern women, entrained to live within a busy and masculine-energy world, the rarified worlds of the original temple priestesses of the love goddess seem a million miles away, and we are more familiar with the ways feminine energy has been prostituted or devalued.

But a renaissance is underway, as the feminine spirit is returning through ordinary woman and spirit weavers across the world. Our inner priestess brings us back into true balance, back into our bodies, deep into our hearts and soul, giving us the light of our desires as a way shower.

We can choose to slow down, reconnect, and reclaim the throne of our own inner temples.

 ### Reclaim Your Holy Whore: One-Hour Ritual

꩜ Buy or craft an organic herbal body oil infused with herbs such as mugwort or rose.

꩜ Spend twenty minutes massaging this oil into your body with sacred intentions and prayers.

꩜ Spend twenty minutes dancing, breathing, or moving your body so the oils can absorb.

꩜ Rinse the oil off your body, anoint yourself with essential oils, and meditate for twenty minutes.

Resources

Menee's article, "Sacred Prostitutes and Temple Slaves: The 'Sexual Priestesses' of Aphrodite," was self-published in an online journal that is no longer available. Her work is referenced in Budin, Stephanie. *The Myth of Sacred Prostitution in Antiquity*. New York: Cambridge University Press, 2008.

THIRTY-SEVEN

PRINCE OF SCORPIO

The Dancing Magician

On the path of feminine magic, you will meet our dear old friend the trickster, who will doff his black top hat to you, stretch out his elegant hand, and invite you to dance into a deeper magic.

Across all magical traditions, a trickster figure is central to the story lore. In some traditions this is the spirit of coyote or the wily fox or wolf. Sometimes this being can be playful, tricky, mischievous, tripping us up and teaching us something about our own unknown dark side. Sometimes this figure can be presented as something more sinister. Either way, the trickster figure is central to the path of magic and cannot be painted away with rainbows of light.

On the path of feminine magic I follow, in the awenydd tradition, the trickster is a *magician,* an amoral being who is a teacher and guide, and is woven into the feminine, lunar mysteries. This figure, who can shape-shift between gender, often appears as a male magician and is a counterpoint to the all-good solar hero or king of traditional lore. The magician has studied on the dark side of the moon and has its secrets to share, if you prove yourself worthy of the hidden wisdom. Trickster is also an aspect of the crone and can appear as a wicked old witch.

The trickster magician is often connected with menarche and coming-of-age rites, that liminal moment when we discover our sexuality and awaken

---

In memoriam to the artist Prince, on his death on the Scorpio full moon, 2016.

our womb power. This is reflected in tales of little Red Riding hood and the wicked wolf who shape-shifts into both man and grandmother. In Celtic lore we meet the faerie king who is known to abduct young maidens into his magical faerie world, promising to enthrone her as the faerie queen, with intimations of initiation.

Feminine magic is full of the mischief of the trickster, and in faerie lore, most beings have this dual nature: they can trick or treat you, depending on how cunning and prepared you are and if they like you. That's why there is so much superstition about not meddling with the faeries. There's no such thing as a free ride or someone who's always "nicey-nice" in the magical world.

In awenydd tradition we have the magician Gwydion, brother of Arianhrod, who lives in this magical space of being either dangerous or benevolent and who is intimately connected with the moon mysteries and the magician's apprenticeship inside the spinning tower of Arianhrod.

The archetype of the magician is in low supply these days or suffers many poor imitations.

Which is why on a Scorpio moon in 2016, the collective feminine went into mourning upon the news that Prince had left our world. He was the great trickster magician of our modern age.

How many women wept for Prince on that Scorpio moon? How incredible that he rode home to the spirit world on a wave of deep feminine gratitude and remembrance. He was the archmagician of music and dance who initiated women across the globe with his purple world of wisdom.

As a teenager, in a world of concrete suburbs and polite conversations, Prince roared into my psyche on his purple motorbike with revelations of erotic promise and sexual power.

He didn't make women want to have sex; he made women want to *be* sex. He opened a forbidden doorway into the Red River of alluring eroticism, where nothing would ever be safe again, but everything would be dangerously alive.

He was a cosmic dancing trickster, who had the keys to open Pandora's secret box. He was a man who knew how to become the moon.

In ancient Sumeria and Babylon, the moon was known as a man called Sin, who wooed women.

Prince was charged with a sensual female power that knew how to drive her magical "Little Red Corvette." There was anguish too, not just a slick sexual superficiality. He channeled the pain of the world soul, lamenting "When Doves Cry." Five feet tall and drenched in sequins, hairspray, and eyeliner, he had more wild erotic masculinity pouring through one spin of a well-turned heel than any man I knew. He embodied the fluid, changing, erotic allure of moonlight.

According to cultural critic Nancy J. Holland, in "Purple Passion: Images of Female Desire," Prince brought the sense of the sexual uncanny to his music, an evocation of a long-forgotten female sexuality, as if he held the priestess codes. She wrote: "The uncanny code constitutes a counter-code to the usual male-oriented sexuality of rock music and represents an attempt to elicit a non-stereotypical female sexuality—female desire outside of the male sexual economy."

I wept for Prince when he passed to Arianhrod's tower—but not really for him. I didn't know him. I wept for myself and for the magical world he represented and for the part of me that still serenades my feminine soul with the words: "I only want to see you dancing in the purple rain."

May he dance with the dakinis as he returns to the "Great Red Corvette" in the sky.

Resources

Holland, Nancy J. "Purple Passion: Images of Female Desire in 'When Doves Cry.'" *Cultural Critique,* no. 10 (1988): 89–98.

THIRTY-EIGHT

ECSTATIC MYSTICS

The Passion of Teresa of Ávila

I was percolating on my long-standing knowing that the energy that Saint Teresa of Ávila was connecting to was not necessarily the straitlaced God as religious folk see him but the cosmic trickster—the archetypal universal principle of the sacred masculine polarity.

Often, especially in old Europe, everyday folk prayed to Jesus *and* the faeries, and Jesus as a liminal, talismanic being became entwined with Pan or the faerie king, the lord of magic. Female mystics opened to this lunar lover aspect of the lord with wild passion and devotion.

Following an ancient path of mysticism, I sense that Teresa's passion for Christ combined a kundalini awakening alongside humility and dedication to the creator, becoming a gateway to ecstatic god consciousness and the high Womb enlightenment of the feminine mysteries.

During this percolation, I opened a book on Teresa of Ávila, edited by Mirabai Starr, and it fell open to the page where Teresa is longing for and lamenting for union with her "lover" Jesus. She calls him a "Supreme Trickster" as she chastises him for abandoning her once again and leaving her in a state of wild desire.

> *O Lord, you Supreme Trickster! What subtle artfulness you use to do your work in this slave of yours. You hide yourself from me and afflict me with your love. You deliver such a delicious death that my soul would never dream of trying to avoid it.*
>
> TERESA OF ÁVILA, *THE BOOK OF MY LIFE*

Every time she mentions Jesus or the Lord, the trickster is winking out from the page, tipping his top hat mischievously, and shimmering with cosmic erotic divine allure.

The essence and wording of her laments are identical in energy to the bhakti poets of Bengal who have given themselves to the ravishment of the divine love of Radha and Krishna, such as Chandidas, one of the poet-saints I particularly love. He describes divine love as "that terrible love . . . as the fire encircled me."

Also in Hindu mythology we find Kama Devi—the primordial god of longing and desire. He is represented as a young and handsome man who wields a bow and arrow, which pierces the heart with primal eros and desire. His arrows are decorated with five types of fragrant flowers, including the blue lotus and white lotus flowers.

Similarly, in Greece the god of love is Eros (or Cupid in Roman lore) who also uses his bow and arrow to pierce the heart and womb of lovers with primordial longing for union and connection.

Is it any coincidence that Teresa describes an angelic god of love, whose erotic arrows set her on fire with divine love and longing and place her in a long lineage of tantric mysteries, which also include the cult of Orpheus and the path of Aphrodite as the great goddess of love?

Teresa goes on to describe one of her highest communions with God, where a beautiful male angel appears substantiated in her room, by her bed. He looks at her with a divine penetrating gaze and then "plunges his arrow" into her womb, thrusting it deep in and out until she reaches the wildest ecstasy of divine love she has known.

Interestingly, the translation can be either heart or womb, but for reasons of decorum, most translators use the word *heart*. When the true translation of womb is used, it becomes clear what kind of union is happening in that bedroom and that Teresa is in the wild sexual ecstasy of womb awakening!

The saint then goes on to describe how the path to union with God is a dual path of humility and introspection (white river) and holy passion (red river). She is reflecting the theme of this threshold meeting point of chaotic, out-of-control erotic desire (mischievously provided by the cosmic lover or divine trickster), which takes us into the wild. And the harmony and integrity of Ma'at, the goddess of creation, where we experience balance, integration, deep maternal love, and true justice.

One without the other is incomplete; the whore and the mother must merge and become one. Uniting the energy streams of the wild eros of the passionate red river and the nurturing, ethical, and compassionate love of the white river.

So as you dance with the trickster or Pan to open the forbidden gateways of your power and desire, know that you are in good company with the saints, who have also walked this moonlit path of ecstatic awakening into unified divine love.

Magic Weaving

Contemplate these primordial archetypes of white magic and dark, or red, magic, which follow the round dance of the moon. One essence waxes within us, bringing brightness and illumination, full of benevolence and blessings, compassionate and full of abundance and creative energy. The other wanes and dissolves the light into the dark mystery of the night and the path of eros, initiation, magic, death, and rebirth. When these forces balance within us, true alchemical wisdom is revealed and embodied. Do you feel called to embody more white magic or dark/red magic?

Ma'at—Goddess of Balance: Guardian of the White River

Holding, nurturing, full moon, conception (holding a child), justice, balance
Meditate on these essences and explore if they are present in your life or desires:

> Forgiveness

> Contentment

> Sharing your gifts

> Mothering yourself

Trickster—Spirit of Initiation: Guardian of the Red River

Releasing, initiating, dark moon, menstruation (death and rebirth), transformation

Meditate on these essences and explore if they are present in your life or desires:

☽ Passion

☽ Transformation

☽ Release and letting go

☽ Awakening your sexuality

Resources

Chandidas. *Love Songs of Chandidas: Rebel Poet-Priest of Bengal.* Translated by Deben Bhattacharya. New York: Grove Press, 1970.

Teresa of Ávila. *Teresa of Ávila: The Book of My Life.* Translated by Mirabai Starr. Boston: New Seeds, 2007.

THIRTY-NINE

METATRON MAGIC

Dragons of Creation

Dragon energy is primal life force energy. In many ancient cultures the telluric earth energy that flows through Gaia and the human body (also a piece of earth) and the cosmos is called a dragon or serpent. The ancient dragon mothers and their twin flame consorts hold the primordial blueprints of creation and birth and dissolve worlds together. One of the more well-known dragon mothers is Metatron (often visualized as a male angel!). *Metatron* is another word for the Shekinah, the in-dwelling presence of God and the Womb of the mystery. This is the intelligence that builds creation, the indwelling spirit of dark matter, and is also sometimes known as Matronit (Mother). It is the creative mother spirit at the root of the universe.

Interestingly, science now shows that after the big birth, creation was formed by twin particles.

This feminine spirit is mythically visioned as a dragon but is practically expressed as universal templates or sacred geometries. Metatron, the dragon mother-father, is also closely connected with the universal blueprints of creation such as Metatron's cube and the Flower of Life (a complex pattern of overlapping circles that creates flower shapes and portals). These Womb grids or portals form the basis of all life. Visualizing and meditating on this geometry helps restore the original dragon codes and awaken our creative powers and regenerative capacity.

These patterns are found across all cultures, from Flower of Life mandalas carved on ancient temples in Sumeria and India to the beautiful biomorphic patterns depicted in Islamic art.

These geometries are also potently concentrated in the Womb, which holds our primordial birthing templates, and the ancient dragon mothers are most intimately supportive of waking the Womb dragon within and reactivating the original intelligence of the womb space.

In some ways, you could say that Metatron delivered my womb "wake-up call."

Like many of us, when I reflect back on my life, I can see I was walking the path of feminine magic all along. It was a secret I was guarding and carrying so tightly that even I didn't see it. Then, one day, this secret path of magic spirituality ambushed me and outed itself in my life.

While I was getting a massage at my local yoga center, the masseur suggested I go to an event the next day. It was a meditation circle dedicated to the Angel Metatron. I was aghast at the thought of it, as I was not interested in channeled angels or such-like at the time.

But of course, intrigued and curious, I went to receive this transmission from Metatron.

As soon as the meditation began, I felt myself falling backward into a huge crystal prism, faceted with many different dimensions of light and color, dancing in fractals of pulsing geometry. The overall feeling was a sense of an immense feminine presence, weaving and creating, pulsing magic in and out of the world, and holding it all inside her womb world.

Afterward, as many people shared their stories of a handsome male angel (unfortunately, I never got to meet him), I kept silent about my own feminine vision that was pulsing within every cell of my body. It was as if dragon's fire had been breathed inside me, and my womb was alive.

Meditating on these sacred geometries of the primal structures of the dragon womb of the universe can awaken our own feminine magic within and thread us back into the weave of life.

 *Metatron and Flower of Life Meditation*

☽ Sit with your hands on your womb space.

☽ Gaze softly at the Flower of Life mandala.

☽ Begin to vision it within your own womb space.

☽ Then gently close your eyes and sit for ten minutes.

FORTY

Quantum Leaps

The Mysteries of Time

On magical paths, we often learn to access realms that are beyond time and space—the seed space of creation, the formless, the infinity, the great void. There is great power and benefit in this. But in feminine mystery teachings, we are also working with flow or the power of shakti, which is embodied here within time and space. So we learn the magical art of working with the power of time. Time itself is a magical being and is not limited to our ideas of it.

We currently live in a man-made time dictated by our man-made clocks. Time is not what we ordinarily think of as time—as just some kind of mechanical function of the universe or ultimately as an illusion. Instead, we begin to think of time as a cosmic intelligence in its own right. Time is a dragon of creation and is highly conscious and relational; time exists, but it is not mechanical or static. It speeds up, it slows down, it has openings, it responds to us. When we understand and connect with the dragons of time, we can travel and transform the time lines.

Astrology is a big part of this magical practice, as the way time moves through these cycles has different qualities and essences. One of our ancestors' major preoccupations was understanding the cyclical nature of time and the intelligence of time and making the most of these auspicious nodes of time. There is a sacred ceremonial landscape of time that weaves the cosmos together.

For instance, our ancestors built megalithic temples to use these passages of time, understanding the concept that we have to know when to flow with life and know what the intelligence of life is saying to us, both collectively in the astrological or lunar-solar planetary phases and also in our inner planetary phases.

There are times, if we compare time to traffic, when time is flowing fast for you and you need to align with that flow, that speed, that spontaneity to not get left behind. At other times, time is slower, like a traffic jam, and you need to learn patience and pacing, to flow and weave, to spot the opening and instinctively take it with grace, and also to spot the obstructions or the difficult areas and avoid them.

Time is the most magical dimension of our lives. The Bible taught that there is a time for everything, a time to sow and a time to reap. To really be working with the flow of time, sometimes in your life you have a green light: you may feel that there is massive flow of synchronicity, the sense that the universe, the feminine wisdom, is saying go. This is the time to move and start projects and relationships and really surf that wave of time that's flowing you to a new dimension of being. If you don't catch that flow, you've missed an important opportunity.

Other times you get an amber light, which is the sense that things are kind of moving but it's a waiting time, so you have to learn to wait and trust the process of waiting.

And sometimes you get a red light, where everything is stuck and stopped. Again, you have to learn to trust that as part of the cycle and not move when the universe is giving you the signal to stop. If you try to push against that, you will come out of the flow of life—in the same way that if you don't move when the green light is flashing, you will come out of the flow of life.

But the dragon of time can help you—if you call upon her.

 ## *Meditation: Meeting the Dragon of Time*

☽   Sit quietly with one hand on your womb space and one hand on your heart.

☽   Begin to follow the rhythm of your breathing—noticing the in breath and the out breath.

- Slowly allow yourself to become aware of the presence of time.

- Feel how each breath is flowing you down a river of energy called time.

- Allow the river of time to eddy into a small spiral pool, swirling in a vortex.

- Allow yourself to be gently drawn down into that vortex. Where do you arrive?

- You are now outside of time as you know it. You see a large dragon eye open.

- Keep breathing and opening and allow the dragon of time to transmit wisdom to you.

The key principle of feminine magic is flowing with the forces of life and the personal, planetary, and cosmic cycles. Learn to listen, trust, and move with them.

> *There is a time for everything, and a season for every activity under the heavens: a time to be born and a time to die, a time to plant and a time to uproot, a time to kill and a time to heal, a time to tear down and a time to build, a time to weep and a time to laugh, a time to mourn and a time to dance, a time to scatter stones and a time to gather them, a time to embrace and a time to refrain from embracing, a time to search and a time to give up, a time to keep and a time to throw away, a time to tear and a time to mend, a time to be silent and a time to speak, a time to love and a time to hate, a time for war and a time for peace.*
>
> ECCLESIASTES

Enchanting Our World

FORTY-ONE

Eclipse Magic

The Lion and the Mermaids

This was written with Azra Bertrand during the Grand Solar Eclipse of 2017, which passed very close to where we live. In articles written in 2017, astrologers speculated on what this "Grand American Eclipse" might bring. Previous astrological events had often brought spiritual darkness. A similar eclipse occurred at the start of the American Revolution in 1776, and the last eclipse of this kind over America—a hundred years ago, in 1918—presided over a World War and the Spanish flu pandemic, which killed millions. Looking back now, these predictions bring an eerie forewarning. But there is more to this than meets the eye. Eclipse magic brings chaos and rebirth. This event also ushered in the return of the archetypal mermaids and lions of love. The Sabian astrological symbol for this portentous Leo solar eclipse was that of a mermaid emerging from the ocean waves, ready for rebirth in human form. It represents the balance of feminine and masculine, and the alchemical fusion of fire and water. Eclipses are portals of healing magic. Back then we wrote . . .

We are about to experience a solar eclipse that is a portal to a paradigm shift. On the waves of lunar consciousness come the rise of the mermaids, the feminine water bearers of wisdom and the awakening of the fiery heart of the lion into his passion.

The total solar eclipse in Leo, on August 21, 2017, is an extremely potent astrological event that heralds the return of mystical feminine consciousness and the rebirth of the ancient mermaid priestesses. In every sense, the moon is about to eclipse the sun.

The burning heat of the hypermasculine paradigm is about to be tamed by love.

It is a gateway of the Grail.

Sacred Union of the Moon and the Sun

The Sabian astrological symbol for this 29-degree Leo eclipse is "a mermaid emerges from the ocean waves ready for rebirth in human form," confirming that the mermaid priestesses are returning to the planet after a long and difficult absence. Women are remembering their power, and their feminine divinity. Above all else, this eclipse is a gateway of feminine activation, transmitting the energetic codes that will help women awaken to the mystical power of their wombs, and rebirth the ancient priestess arts.

This eclipse is also a gateway of sacred union. Powerful masculine and feminine symbols are conjoined: the sun with the moon and the feminine Aquarius, bearing her watery womb chalice, with the masculine lion of Leo. The brightest star in the constellation of Leo is Regulus, the "heart of the lion" and one of the four Royal Stars that serve as guardians of the night sky. Leo represents the spiritual purification of the masculine heart and is a vision keeper of the highest frequencies of love in action, one that honors and protects the feminine—the lion of love.

Divine Feminine Mermaids and Lions of Love

Back in 2016, I [Azra] had a vivid dream, which I now understand to be a foreshadowing of this important eclipse. I was in a majestic forest, with cathedrals of trees reaching up to the skies. The forest extended to the edge of a cliff before dropping down into a beautiful bay below. I could sense the presence of mermaids in the waters, as well as ancient whales, turtles, and dolphins swimming in these waters of life. But I could also feel a danger approaching and that the creatures within it needed to be protected.

Out of my peripheral vision I sensed a movement in the woods. Looking up, I saw a group of white lions bounding toward me from a distance, emanating an energy of wild power. A wave of fear washed through as I understood they were coming for me. My rational mind said "Run!" But in my heart I knew I needed to commune with these beings.

As they neared me, the white lions slowed to a trot and gracefully approached. The lead male lion looked with deep intensity into my eyes and began communicating to me telepathically. "You are here to remind women that they are mermaids. You must help them remember. The fate of our Earth depends on it. Do you understand?"

I nodded, communicating that I clearly understood their message. The white lion held my gaze for a few more moments before bounding off again into the woods. My entire being was charged with purpose—my mission was to help awaken the mermaids.

This confirmed what I already knew; men are also an essential part of the fabric of this grand shift, with a powerful sacred purpose of their own as protectors of the Grail of Life.

 ## Eclipses Are Celestial Gateways

Throughout time, people have known the power and significance of total eclipses. Solar eclipses always bring powerful shifts in consciousness. They are celestial gateways that mark the end of one era and beginning of the next. The 2017 eclipse was especially potent, as it brings in the next wave of evolution since the long-prophesied 2012 sacred feminine birthing portals opened to simultaneously end multiple great cycles, including a 66-million-year evolutionary age, a 26,000-year precessional age, and the 2,000-year age of Pisces, as Earth now moves into the sign of Aquarius, the feminine water bearer.

During this eclipse, the new moon will completely obscure the light of the midday sun, casting her primordial lunar darkness along a path extending from one coast of America to the other. Energetically this represents the rise of the mystical feminine lunar consciousness, bringing balance to the earth after a long period of patriarchal solar domination. It is an inherently intense time, a time of spiritual death and rebirth.

The last total solar eclipse of this magnitude happened in 1776, the year that the United States declared its independence from Great Britain. Looking back further in time, a total solar eclipse was recorded nearly two thousand years ago, at the exact moment that Yeshua (Jesus) spiritually died and rebirthed through the womb cross or Tree of Life of the feminine.

 A Total Eclipse of the Womb

In an amazing synchronicity, *Womb Awakening* was conceived during the 2012 cosmic portal of the sacred feminine and is now being birthed during this total solar eclipse gateway. We first begin writing in earnest during our time living in Cornwall, near the Zennor Mermaid, and the book is a modern-day mystery text encoded with the lost teachings of the Womb priestesses, also known as the mermaids, sirens, or Magdalenes.

Our book *Womb Awakening* [and also *Magdalene Mysteries*] remembers the resurrection rituals of the mermaid priestesses, with symbolic messages to help women and men awaken to the mystical lunar consciousness of the Womb and the grail codes of creation. It could not have been more perfectly orchestrated with these greater celestial movements if we had tried, and looking back, we can see very clearly that there was a greater current of energy flowing through, coordinating it all in a way that was beyond our understanding at the time.

Our deepest desire is to midwife the rebirth of the mermaids.

The world needs a miracle right now, and that miracle will birth through the feminine.

May the moon and the sun be one.

Ritual for Solar or Lunar Eclipse Events

☽ Sit in Womb meditation and ask what three things you are birthing.

☽ Sit in Womb meditation and ask what three things you are dissolving.

☽ Write an eclipse vision statement for your life and the world.

☽ Make sure you hold a sacred energy for the two hours around the eclipse.

☽ Make sure you are not in an environment that triggers your or others' shadows.

☽ If you can, craft a Womb medicine pouch to store your written intentions.

☽ Place pictures of mermaids or white lions on your altar, computer screen, or in your social media.

FORTY-TWO

ᴅʀᴇᴀᴍ Wɪsᴅᴏᴍ

Awakening the Psyche

Our deep feminine psyche is the birther and creator of our life and experience. Our conscious cerebral mind is the translator but not the birther. Our inner world—also known as the Otherworld—plants the seeds, and our mind puts them into action.

In magical feminine wisdom, it was known that to change anything we had to change our dream time first. To dream a new dream, we had to begin in the Otherworld within, what science calls the quantum realm. Actions on the outer world had more limited outcomes. Only when we changed our dreams, which birth our waking life, could true transformation begin.

Ancient shamans believed there were entities who had hijacked our psyche. They believed these entities lived deep within our psyche and fed us, manipulated dreams as we slept, which we then lived out in reality. Often we were unaware of the dark dreams that we had experienced as we slept and their toxic consequences. Instead, we would wake up feeling out of sorts and go on to re-create suffering.

We can also extend this analogy to entities in the collective psyche. These nefarious energies feed us a subconscious nightmare that we then birth into reality.

This knowledge was the basis of mastering dream-time magical skills. By bringing the dream time into consciousness and entering the feminine psyche to confront the demons held within, we could also recover our soul treasures.

These dream-time magical arts included recalling dreams, lucid dreaming, dreaming awake, and psychic journeying. A simple practice to begin with is to bring the dreams and nightmares of the psyche into consciousness by writing down our dreams in a dream journal. The more we actively recall our experiences in the dream-time Otherworld, the more access we have to our lost psychic realms.

Psychic journeying through enchanted magic doorways can also help us enter the feminine realms. The more we take these journeys within and allow ourselves to open the doorways of our soul, the more love can stream through to us.

With enough expertise, we can begin to engage with our Otherworld psyche in lucid ways. What this means is we can begin to heal our psyche at a deep root level and transform our foundational birthing field into one of love rather than suffering. We can start to develop a conscious co-creative relationship with our feminine self.

A more modern way of viewing these entities is to see them as past traumas and emotional wounds. These experiences, which the conscious mind has skipped over and forgotten about, live on deep in our feminine psyche and effectively take over as we enter the dream world, crying out for us to remember this hidden pain.

These dream-time entities are also formed from our ancestral legacy, remembered in our "dark" DNA. Often the monsters of the deep in our psyche represent something much deeper than our own personal memories and lives. They are an amalgamation of our ancestors, parallel lives, and the collective memory. The psyche is nonlogical and nonlinear and is not measured by time as we know it.

Redreaming our feminine psyche back to wholeness is the key to conscious manifestation. When we undertake the grail quest and journey into our feminine self, our Otherworld psyche—also called the subconscious and unconscious—we create deep healing that lasts and that transforms the circumstances of our lives.

Underneath the demons and nightmares of our forbidden psyche lives an enchanted realm of innocence. This immaculate consciousness is within us all along and is the foundation of who we are. She is calling to us to redream ourselves and our world. To birth from our love and beauty, not the fear-field of past trauma.

The queendom of feminine consciousness is calling us home.

When we undertake this journey into our lost feminine psyche, we reclaim our true self. We remember how beautiful and magical we are and how we were born to live from this truth. As we embody this healing, we become a grail light of the world.

> *It is no secret. All power is one in source and end, I think. Years and distances, stars and candles, water and wind and wizardry, the craft in a woman's hand and the wisdom in a tree's root: they all arise together. My name, and yours, and the true name of the sun, or a spring of water, or an unborn child, all are syllables of the great word that is very slowly spoken by the shining of the stars. There is no other power. No other name.*
> URSULA K. LE GUIN, *A WIZARD OF EARTHSEA*

FORTY-THREE

SOUL ALCHEMY

Merging Power and Love

Alchemy is the magical art of fusion within the psyche and within our creative energy fields. This coming together creates a spontaneous evolution of new possibilities and births a divine child, in much the same way that a man and woman coming together in union can birth a baby. Our consciousness is rebirthed.

In alchemical individuation we merge the opposing forces of our inner energy and desires, often expressed as fire and water or masculine and feminine. The alchemical marriage is often described as setting fire to water. In the mystical Jewish tradition of kabbalah, expressed in the kabbalistic Tree of Life, the right column of Chesed (opening with an outpouring of unconditional love) is balanced with the left column of Guverah (boundaries or conditions that awaken our power). It can also be expressed as a unification of the white river with the red river.

In practical terms, this reflects our need to balance our desire to open our hearts to others in unconditional love and understanding, with the need to maintain our own personal power and boundaries, which protect and guide us through our life. Inside the friction of these desires, we find our greatest paradox as humans: we are unlimited, unconditional beings, who have the power to apply conditions and limits. On Earth we are eternal beings having a limited experience. Alchemy seeks to unite these opposing desires into complementary teammates.

Vicki Noble says of alchemy: "In Tarot tradition, the Temperance card represents the empowerment of Alchemy, the process of blending the parts of the self until fusion is achieved and the 'philosopher's stone' is made. This also refers to the culmination of shamanic initiation, and integration of the emotional forces."

Medieval alchemists were dedicated to birthing a golden consciousness. This awakened consciousness was key to living in harmony with one another and Earth. Their wisdom sought to preserve a prehistoric religion, which understood the need to balance the incredible spectrum of our infinite emotions and desires as human beings with the reality of living in physical forms on a planet with finite resources. Alchemy is rooted in this deep understanding of Earth magic.

In alchemical traditions the goddess Ma'at and the principle of Ma'at also embodies this mystical marriage. Ma'at is also symbolized by the astrological sign of Libra and the scales of justice, which are constantly tipping from one end to the other. In Egyptian lore, only those whose heart is light as a feather, who have balanced the opposites perfectly to embody divine order and justice, can enter heavenly realms. This divine harmony is a psychological state of unification, which births the consciousness of innocence, where all transgressions are forgiven and integrated. When we are "out of Ma'at" we are no longer living within the laws of creation.

The Ma'at mythology can be divined as the alchemical depth journey of the psyche.

The founders of modern psychology also drew inspiration from the ancient art of alchemy and this tantric fusion of our lunar and solar selves. They expressed this in psychological terms as the merging of our oral baby self and our sexual teenage self through a process of individuation and psychic integration. This individuation marries our personal power to our interpersonal love and does not separate them.

We first experience this interpersonal and symbiotic unconditional love as a baby growing in the womb of our mother and suckling on her breast. This is a heart-centered time of unconditional love. As an adult, as our sexual creative power awakens, we then individuate into a separate being with our own personal boundaries and desires that comes from our own creative resources. This is a time of conditions and exploring what boundaries and limits to apply.

In ancient and indigenous societies, rites of passage—to mark, birth, menstruation, and coming of age—were the key to helping the psyche to adapt to new stages of consciousness. It was known that without marking these important thresholds symbolically, in ritual, the psyche would not be able to individuate into maturity.

As a baby, numerous rituals from preconception to conception, gestation, birth, and postbirth helped a new baby adjust to life on Earth. He or she received her own soul song, and the placenta was buried in the earth so that a deep umbilical connection was created between the baby and the Earth Mother who would feed, clothe, warm, and protect the baby during its life and take him or her back upon death.

This helped the baby feel safe and held during this delicate period of dependency, where the baby is reliant on the birth mother's love and care for its very survival.

A person experienced their second birth during their teenage years, usually around the age of thirteen, when they came of age and physically matured into creative beings who could seed or birth a new human life and seed and birth other energetic creations. For a girl, this was marked by celebrations of her first menstruation. For a boy, this was marked by rites of passage that initiated him into his manhood—teaching him maturity, self-responsibility, and the consequences of his actions.

In childhood, we discover the unconditional love of the mother, and in our coming of age, as a teenager, we meet the limiting force of the father, who constricts us so that we can grow and find our way in the world and coexist with others. These are genderfluid ideas, and interestingly in the kabbalah, it is the father who is unlimited love and the mother who represents boundaries and limitations, just as the womb is an alchemical chamber with boundaries. In tarot lore, it is the cup of love that nourishes us and the sword of power that prunes us. As any gardener knows, fertile soil and wise pruning bloom the garden.

We see how in the modern world, without any rites of passage or knowledge of alchemical principles, a state of psychic disintegration occurs. The world is full of wounded babies living in adult bodies and sexual desires disconnected from love or appropriate boundaries. Some have never managed to grow up and own their power or creativity, and others have broken the umbilical cord of connection to achieve a false power in separation from mother consciousness.

Alchemical individuation is when our child consciousness, formed in the root of the motherworld, grows toward the sunlight to express itself uniquely and bloom into a beautiful flower, without disconnecting from the mother root that created it.

This connection is held within the archetypal Great Mother, who lives as the essence of all birth mothers (who are not always able to embody their own mother essence).

We know the truth of our symbiosis with the Great Mother and the web of life, while also birthing the unique creative power of our own wildness, passion, desire, and longing.

Psychic alchemy is not achieved by separating or individuating away from either pole of energy but by the unification of the two complementary forces at the heart of life. When our infinite love and our embodied power marry, a new divine child of potential births.

This is a collective energy field of consciousness that transforms us, restores us, and allows us to have the maturity to wield our power wisely and become adult co-creators with life—rather than spiritual adolescents who trash the earth as if we are ungrateful teenagers throwing a party in our parents' house. Or unhealed children who must depend entirely on others to survive.

Awakening invites us to grow up, to bloom, to fulfill our true creative potential.

> *I celebrate myself and sing myself,*
> *And what I assume you shall assume,*
> *For every atom belongs to me as good belongs to you.*
>
> WALT WHITMAN, FROM "SONG OF MYSELF"

Resources

Noble, Vicki. *Motherpeace: A Way to the Goddess through Myth, Art, and Tarot.* New York: HarperOne, 1994.

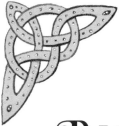

FORTY-FOUR

Biology of Bonding

Sacred Union and Soulmates

I often find that it is controversial to talk about soulmates within the spiritual world, as it is often viewed as wrong and unspiritual to seek anything outside yourself or to feel incomplete in any way.

Yet one of the deepest journeys I have been on is rediscovering this foundational longing to bond and merge and connect and all the ways I have shut this down to fit in with a culture that fiercely promotes independence. Opening to interconnection and the qualities of natural dependence it brings can be terrifying and overwhelming. The idea of having a "twin" also means becoming *entwined*—it suggests a weaving together of two separate beings into a magical third. The relationship is actually an energy field that creates a new world and weaves our hearts together.

As a single woman and career girl for over a decade, who had a successful job, owned my own house, traveled alone, and didn't need anyone, marriage was quite an adjustment.

Riane Eisler talks about this subject in her brilliant book *Sacred Pleasure,* describing how the feminine dimension of experience, such as needs, dependence, nurturing, connectivity, and bonding, is ruthlessly devalued to promote hypermasculine concepts of independence, fearlessness, not needing, and self-containment. This bias filters all the way down into our psychological systems and our spiritual systems, whether we are conscious of it or not.

This unconscious yet dangerous bias is at the root of many of the ills of the world today. We are not taught to value or experience mutual relationship or fully understand or respect our deep interdependency with Earth, or others.

The magnitude of this was brought home to me as I began to explore the actual structure of our psychology and biology. Through explorations with Azra Bertrand, who has studied the human psycho-bioenergetic system for many years and was involved in primary research at the NIH on mother-baby bonding and its impact on the endocrine system, I came to understand the devastating consequence of diminishing the realities of the feminine dimension of Earth.

When we deny the true needs of our body, heart, and soul, our psyche fragments and develops defense structures that are not rooted in reality. Our body's healthy mechanisms of healing and happiness start to break down and self-destruct. Collectively, this is also now happening to us as a species, as our mass defense structures of distraction begin to threaten the deep-feminine ecosystem system of Earth.

In our book *Womb Awakening,* we also explore these issues and delve into a feminine-centric approach to modern sacred relationship with our beloveds and with Earth itself.

We highlight the importance of holding open our hearts for the possibility of a soulmate—literally, the mate or twin of our soul. The person (of any gender) who complements us and holds us in love so we can dismantle any damaging defense structures and come back to our vulnerable heart; the lover who brings us back down to the realm of earth—with all its complexities, challenges, and primal beauty.

To meet and merge with our soulmate, we also have to discover, explore, and awaken our own inner soul. Because how can our true soul meet its mate if it we have lived our lives without really knowing our own depths and desires and potential and without embodying our own soul power?

Ultimately, we are twinned with everything. Try going for one moment without food, water, oxygen, gravity, light, heat, shelter, and a multitude of other important biological factors that we are not even aware of. We do so at our own peril. And these are just the obvious physical examples, for our soul biology also needs love, connection, touch, listening, holding, beauty, elemental infusions, moonlight, and the subtle energies transmitting from the cosmos and the Earth Womb.

This is a realm of soul-mate magic calling us home.

FORTY-FIVE

OPENING TO LOVE

Descending into the Heart

Opening to love is the initiation of Ascension.
Paradoxically, this journey first invites us into a radical descension.
We cannot open our wings until we have found our roots.
You will know when you have met this initiatory love.

I had thought I had at least faced, if not healed, the main source of my wounds in order to meet and unite with my beloved—the other particle of me.

Yet I was to discover those previous wounds were only the appetizer. The main course was to come, embedded deep in the roots of union.

It was lived in the day-to-day detail of intimate relationship, where there was no off button, no escape, no romantic getaway. It involved opening to the deepest love that could hold and embrace the anger, the projection, the numbness, the fear and move beyond that into the unfamiliar lands of total ecstasy, bonding, oneness.

It contained the bewildering knowing that true love was our deepest desire—and also our deepest fear. It was like dancing close to a flame and then swirling inside. It would melt you, dissolve you, transform you—but first it would completely illuminate you.

Not just the radiant heart of yourself, your soulful self, but also your deep, unknown, forbidden sexual self and the split part of you that wends like a dark twine around the DNA of Earth, who has been both victim and perpetrator and denies it.

It meant feeling through a Russian doll of past heartbreaks and healing their cellular echo.

I began to understand in Technicolor detail why many people are not in a loving and conscious relationship, even if they say this is what they want more than anything. Only when we desire love and truth more than anything does this true love begin to seek us down. It seeks us when we seek our reality, the raw, unbounded, ecstatic devastation of awakening into our soul self.

It comes when we desire love more than reliving, in a fatalistic loop, the dark fairy story of our childhood that we have spun to protect ourselves and more than the fantasy of our collective history, which has been created to disempower and deny ourselves. It means looking at the disturbing details of our lives, not just the press release story our coping strategies have devised to look good and keep safe.

To truly meet another in the furnace of love, you have to meet yourself.

Often we are led to this place by the sheer exhaustion of the suffering we have created in our lives—twinned with a deep devotional longing to truly be love.

Sacred union is a descent to what we now call hell but was once the shimmering, ecstatic, primordial feminine root of consciousness. It is a journey of courage and utter madness. It is infinitely deep. It expands to include vistas of consciousness, both personal and collective, that we have spent our entire life denying and defending against. Sacred union is a process that brings us to the heart of truth.

Not a fluffy, toothless, spiritual truth.
But something beatific, terrifying, astounding, incandescent, horrifying.

We are shocked by the sight of our own shadow.
We are startled by the light of our own soul.

The word *horror* is a Womb word.
Hor means "cave" or "womb"; *or* means "golden light."

We enter the Womb of light for our death and rebirth initiation.

Relationship, love, sexuality, desire, intimacy open the door wide for us.

It is deep within this vast primordial shining darkness where we meet the truth of our pure essential consciousness and where the web of all our unconscious actions, beliefs, programs, and deceptions are reflected back to us, in order to heal.

In this "horror" of Womb enlightenment, we are greeted by the truth-thirsty Kali within our psyche, who switches on the light of self-knowing to reveal our real self.

We finally see these deep wounds with such clarity that we can kiss them good night.

These patterns are most deeply etched in our relationships—where all our greatest hopes and fears live, where our desires for contact, love, and intimacy simmer away.

In a world of emotional confusion and complexity, love holds a torch of beautiful simplicity.

It reminds us, remembers us, humbles us, brings us back home. The heart becomes a nest of transmutation, velvet lined with soft feathers of hope.

With trust and commitment, a sacred relationship becomes a circle of rebirth.

In a moment, a touch, a kiss, a look, the silken feeling of skin on skin, where boundaries melt, can evaporate all our most cherished beliefs and spiritual theories.

We are naked right down to the bones of our soul, joined together.
We swim oceans of tender innocence, in wild exposure, with audacious bliss.
It is here that the madness and magic of union happens.
In the depth of this Womb of rebirth is a doorway of light.

Love meets us with a soft smile and invites us to let go and relax into the shimmering innocence. She sings us songs, offers flowers to our fragile hearts.

She reminds us we have never left this root of innocence.

When we descend to this foundational unified root together, in a truly sacred relationship, our sexual union opens out into spaciousness and becomes timeless.

We understand that we are not returning to Eden—we have never left Eden. We sense, bodily, that he is a primordial Adam, and she is a primordial Eve. We enter the mystery of the *yab-yum,* the *hieros gamos,* the bridal chamber. It cannot be put into words; it transmits through eyes, through fingertips.

And this ecstasy would be enough, would be worth the entire world . . .

Yet love, winking, once more invites us into the cosmic washing machine of our wounds. Rinse and repeat. To journey the spiral all over again—and again.

Our bodies become the arms of galaxies.
Our hearts become shooting stars.
We are not falling into love.
We are spiraling into love.

FORTY-SIX

ROMANTIC LOVE

A Mystical Spiritual Path

How can romantic relationship be a spiritual path?

We tend to see being spiritual as something we do as a personal inner journey, and our culture, for thousands of years, has presented us with spiritual icons who have walked a path of solitude. Relational issues—such as fears of abandonment, of being smothered, of neediness and clinginess or difficulty with deep intimacy and resistance to feelings of vulnerability—are often sidelined as people open to a path of spiritual awakening. Yet these relational issues, in all their Technicolor glory, are a doorway to the deepest awakening and rebirth of the psyche. Paradoxically, our history of failed relationships, or the core wounds and patterns of our current relationship, are the place where our deepest treasure is held—if we go deep diving into these patterns we would prefer to ignore. What this means is your long list of relational traumas or heartbreak is actually the golden ticket to your liberation and awakening to love. You don't have to be in a current relationship to experience this transmutation of relationship patterns because the alchemy lab is right there within your deepest heart.

Often we carry a lot of shame about our relational patterns, especially in spiritual circles, where the down-and-dirty drama of our personal romantic and sexual stories doesn't feel evolved enough. Yes, we can do a headstand, meditate, spin our chakras, *and* clear dozens of past-life karmic imprints in one sitting—but if someone asks us for a date or our partner triggers us, we regress a few spiritual decades in one nanosecond. Rather than covering this up, or following theories that promote detachment, we can invite this shame for a cup of tea and a chat. This shame is deep medicine. Inside these feelings of shame and vulnerability lives our sacred heart.

This is the beauty of love. It is full of vulnerability, humility, chaos—and this is fuel for rapid growth. As the philosopher Nietzsche says, "One must still have chaos in oneself to be able to give birth to a dancing star."

Our romantic relationships are a birthing portal.

Romantic relationship as an authentic spiritual path has always been known as a fast track for those prepared to enter the crucible. Sacred lovers such as Yeshua and Magdalene remind us of the magnitude of potential for those who alchemize themselves in love's fire. We may like to imagine them as floating around in the "peace that passeth all understanding." But first there is a "passion that passeth all understanding"—and this is full of wildness, chaos, pain, ecstasy, fear, and the commitment and devotion to keep opening.

Placing our intimate relationships at the center of our spiritual altar creates a paradigm shift. Our everyday life becomes the practice. The messy details of our previous relationships become a rosary bead to meditate and pray with, bringing deep alchemical potential. Our heart's longing to be deeply touched by a soulful love that is embodied and lived here in the flesh becomes a beacon of light.

Mary Magdalene was known as the woman who "loved much." With this path, we are not measured by how evolved or enlightened we are or even how perfect our relationships are. We are called into living the question of how much can we open our heart to love.

Despite all the hurts, all the lifetimes of protection, we choose to open to the sun again. Our inner flower, the rose within our spiritual Womb, awakens again.

And the day came when the risk to remain tight in a bud was more painful than the risk it took to blossom.

ANAÏS NIN

Awakening the Heart's Rose

Trace this Venus rose onto a piece of paper. The five-petaled rose is the sigil of the Rose Lineage. On each petal write the following names:

- ☽ The lover who truly broke your heart
- ☽ The lover who taught you boundaries
- ☽ The lover who enchanted your inner maiden
- ☽ The lover who enthroned you as a queen or mother
- ☽ The lover who taught you to love yourself

Sit with this Venus rose of your inner heart petals and meditate and journal on what you have learned from your lovers and reflect how relationships are a deep mystery school of magic.

FORTY-SEVEN

CHRIST MAGIC

The Goddess of Avalon

Christianity is a glass (or chalice) that can either be half full or half empty, depending on what angle you are looking at it from. It is easy to identify the ways it is half empty, lacking in the necessary substance to nourish the people, a poisoned chalice if you will—where we see "through a glass darkly" the birth-light of creation.

As layers of consciousness peel back, we can identify, name, and quote the patriarchal failings of a one-sided religious tower about to topple, with its inherent flaws of misogyny, homophobia, and evangelical conquests of indigenous traditions.

Yet what elixir remains in that half glass, still sweet with the promise of fullness?

The famous quote of Paul from Corinthians "through a glass darkly" refers to the ancient mirrors, which were made of brass, gave an obscure reflection, and needed to be polished to provide a better image. These mirrors were made in Corinth, where Paul was writing. In Greek, this phrase refers to a riddle or enigma—a very feminine sense of a revelation that presents itself in disguise or holds deep-water meanings.

In fact, looking through a mirror was a key symbol of the feminine religions. Mermaids, the priestesses of Mary, were often depicted holding magic mirrors, which were considered to be portals to the Otherworld and reflected divinations.

What if we were to polish that dark glass of religion to reveal the Holy Grail?

There is a lost beauty and wild mystery in this "new" religion, which still has its thirsty roots deep down into the bedrock of the ancient wisdom of the old ways. Maybe it is not an either/or but the *and* that is a bridge between the old and new?

With its eucharists of regenerative wise blood, baptisms of fire and water, chalices of the fountain of life, a descending-and-rising god and his goddess of resurrection, and a message of simplicity, peace of the sacred heart, redemption through love and kindness, and a willingness to be with suffering and to extend a helping hand—is this not a story that can still speak to us today? If told while the "Marys" of the Bible, the forbidden sacred feminine presence, dance the circle around the teller, casting lilies and roses into the crossway for blessings, then yes. Mary Magdalene is extending a wild swan wing to assist us on this rebirth journey.

During our first visit to Charleston, South Carolina, we accidentally come across a historic home that has a display of art. Intrigued, we climb up the narrow wooden stairs to see a room exhibiting a collection of Mary Magdalene art and sculpture. In the middle of the room is a ravishing white sculpture of Mary Magdalene, prostrate, like a goddess. We contemplate how this home of prominent French Protestants from the past, who do not usually subscribe to Magdalene icons, have her on vivid display. These Huguenots who fled France to avoid persecution clearly revere her memory.

That night I have fevered dream, where I am first pronouncing myself a Catholic and then changing my mind and pronouncing myself a Protestant. So I am both.

In waking life, I am neither. But the fragrance of this communion lingers into the day, the call to the hidden mysteries of this religion, which has both destroyed and preserved the ancient pathways, much like the records of the heretic gnostic feminine teachings preserved mainly by those who scribed their denouncement.

Could the poison also point to the antidote? It is common in herbal lore.

Does Mary Magdalene's medicine bear the healing balm and the homeopathic dose?

 ## Sons and Lovers

Whenever I search for the Goddess, I am also led to her sons and lovers.

One night, many years ago, I sat in an old converted English farmhouse, nestled under the sacred Tor of Glastonbury, the Isle of Avalon, and the terraced labyrinth path of the Goddess, who is embodied as a dragon or swan deep within the land.

It is a candlelit evening of Kirtan, singing sacred chants to the divine lovers, Radha and Krishna, whose sacred love mirrors the ecstatic love play of the cosmic deity.

Christianity, at that time, is a religion I have filed into the same drawer as my father's philosophical comment that "women should be seen and not heard."

The atmosphere in the room is soft and bathed with honey light, and I should be melting into the enchanting melodies of the music. But it has been a difficult few months, and my body is tense with tiredness and a mind that has done battle. I now feel aware that I am not in the flow of bhakti—a heart opened with divine essence. I can't keep my eyes closed and fly off into a profound meditation. Instead, I find my gaze wandering around the gathering, with everyone sitting on small meditation cushions, most people with their eyes closed, swaying serenely to the soft chanting.

My attention is drawn to a young woman sitting on a cushion on my left-hand side, and I notice that tears are streaming down her face. These are not tears of joy or ecstasy but tears that flow from a heart surrendering to the pain that has held up its walls for far too long and can no longer take the strain of all that pressure and holding.

I feel for her. In the sensing of her pain, a hard wall within my own heart wobbles: I feel compassion for her, and more to the point an acute awareness of my own pain. And before I know it, from somewhere kept within a place I cannot name, a prayer rises up like a dove in flight right from deep inside my body and forms onto my lips: "Jesus, please open my heart."

I am not speaking to a god but to a close friend. There is an intimacy, a familiarity, as if I reached out to someone I once knew so well. Part of me is shocked by what has just passed through me. Did I really just pray, without irony, to Jesus Christ?

I don't get time to answer because a supernova has just exploded through my heart—as if a flesh organ could unfold out into a prism of expanding rainbow light. Love is pouring through my heart and flowing outward, and I am sobbing with a feeling that is a homecoming, a belonging, once lost, now remembered, embracing me. I want to tell this young woman how much I love her and to reach out and hug her—I want to hug everyone—and I can barely restrain myself from a wildish love splatter.

It continues. The evening ends, and I walk up the stairs pulsing with a crazy love and a ridiculous smile. My heart is melted. I might as well be high on drugs. I cannot contain myself, and I find inexplicable joy in the smallest of details. I feel blessed, grateful, gushing with contentment—like God/dess just glitter-bombed me. I am sharing a room, and I am struggling to contain the overwhelming love I now feel for my roommate, whom I have never met before and who looks at me slightly bemused.

I look out of the window, onto the darkened streets of Avalon—it feels timeless and rich with ancient magic. There is a picture of Krishna propped up by the bed and a small white tea light. With reverence, I light the candle, and the world illuminates. Within the golden flicker of the flame and the velvet darkness behind, I feel held in the perfect moment, peacefully still, nothing to change or do, shimmering with love.

The next morning, I am back to normal but feeling dazed, softer—more here. Surrounded by the iconography of India, I feel slightly sheepish, as if I accidentally had a spiritual one-night stand with a religion that I had barely even dated before. I got it. Radha and Krishna. Jesus and Magdalene. The cosmic couples were one. Here at the throne of the Lady of the Lake, I had discovered that deep in these ancient lands, by her side, was the spirit of the sacred masculine, embodied in Jesus.

It was as if the doorway that had opened briefly at my menarche was unlocked again—and propped open with a friendly invitation, scented with love and kinship.

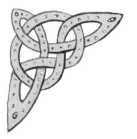

FORTY-EIGHT

Epiphany

Three Wise Witchy Midwives

We often use the word *epiphany* to describe a light-bulb moment when we realize something important that had been hidden away from sight. One of those collective light-bulb moments is tuning into the actual meaning of Epiphany, a celebration that happens thirteen days after Christmas, on January 6. Revered by Celtic Christians, this time honors women's medicine rites. It used to be called Distaff Day, when women began weaving in the new year.

The sacred Christmastime of Epiphany was once the heartland of the feminine mysteries, celebrated by many feminine folk traditions. It celebrated the birth-death-rebirth rites that were practiced by the visionary midwives of consciousness and creation—where the "nativity" of the new birth emerged.

Interestingly, some folklore also speaks of Magdalene having been born on Epiphany, which is known as the Women's Christmas and is a women's celebration day.

The Greek root word for Epiphany, *epifania* or *epiphaenia,* means "appearance" or "manifestation"—connecting it to the creative power of the new birth of light.

Every year, as we enter onto another spiral of life, we are being called to reclaim the sacred feminine essence in our yearly spiritual calendar so we can reconnect and heal. It is a time to awaken and birth the healing fruits of our magical Womb consciousness into the world.

A Shamanic Planetary Descension

In the ancient worlds, and still vibrating in our inner dimensional worlds, the sacred journey between Samhain (October 31) and Imbolc (February 2) was a magical descension journey into the dark Womb of Mother Earth for rebirth and renewal.

This sacred journey was a living mystery play between human beings and the forces of nature—the great elementals and dragons of creation, emissaries of telluric primal energy, whose magic is awake and alive within the human body and psyche yet is also beyond human knowing.

The sacred heart of this shamanic, planetary descension journey unfolds between winter solstice (December 21) and Epiphany (January 6)—as we begin to ascend back into the Upperworld light realms, bringing our "Christed" soul gifts with us.

The eve of Epiphany is known as Twelfth Night (famously encoded by Shakespeare) and is celebrated by revels, feasting, and honorary ritual. In the old ways, a new day started at sunset (not sunrise), as the ancients knew that the womb of darkness always came first. This meant that holy days began on the eve before.

Thirteen Days of Feminine Festivities

On the eve of winter solstice, we enter three days of the dark Womb of the Great Mother, and on the eve of the twenty-fourth and the day of the twenty-fifth, we experience the great rebirth back into the light. This is celebrated for thirteen days (a sacred feminine number) until January 6—now known as Epiphany. In modern religious theology, this holy day is attributed to the journey of the wise men to the nativity of Jesus or to the circumcision of Christ. Traditionally, this thirteen-day period is the time of festivities, celebration, and feasting, associated originally with the Great Mother and the Christmas Witch, linked to Hecate—who administers the sacred birth rites of renewal. Old amulets of Hecate feature the blessing "I am the Resurrection."

The Christmas Witch

In Italian folklore, La Befana is a wise crone archetype of renewal called la Strega Noel, the Christmas Witch, who holds the mythic memories of the witch-priestess tradition of the *strega*—native Italian wise women. It is said she lives in a village on a hill in Via della Padella and is part faerie and part witch. She is described as an old woman wearing the black cape of the initiate and riding a donkey, which is sacred to Egyptian magic.

In Italy, Befana plays a role very similar to Santa Claus; however, instead of a sleigh pulled by reindeer, she flies around on her magical witch's broom and delivers her gifts of either renewed light or the black coal of earth to children on the eve of Epiphany.

Later on, this became connected with her traveling to Jesus's nativity, in a similar way to the three wise men bearing gifts. Along the way, she gives gifts to children. So she becomes the wise midwife of the holy birth.

Shamanic Midwife of Christ

As Christian traditions replaced the feminine shamanic rites, the two stories became entwined in a new mythos, which held clues to the older origins. Later myths describe how the three wise men visited the witch Befana on their way to the nativity of Christ. The kings invite Befana to join them on their journey, telling her they are following a star to navigate their path. Befana replies that she doesn't have time as she is busy sweeping with her broom (feminine magic). As we shall see later, this gives us a knowing wink to the renewal and purification rites of bringing in the new year.

Other variants on the story have Befana changing her mind and jumping on her broomstick to catch up with the three kings. Or, more tellingly, other versions of the folklore say that Befana is summoned to Mother Mary's side to help with the birth and to sweep the stable with her magical broom, possibly a code for midwife rites, which have now been forgotten.

A very curious telling of the tale places Befana in Palestine as a mother living during the time of King Herod. Her male son is one of the children killed in the decree by Herod to prevent the birth of a new savior. In her grief and delusion, she journeys to the crib of Christ and believes that he is her child. Certain that she has found her son, Befana lays out all of her son's belongings for the infant Jesus Christ, who then blesses her as the giver of gifts.

Intuitively, this connects Befana, the Christ witch, not only with the sacred midwife and bearer of gifts but also the Black Madonna—the mother of the Christ light.

Magical Night of Renewal

As mentioned previously, la Befana is also linked to the goddess Hecate, who is part of a triple form of the Goddess of the moon mysteries. Interestingly, this triple aspect of feminine wisdom associated with the renewal rites of Epiphany was appropriated to three men.

Epiphany, known as a night of magic, was once an important sacred feminine holy time. Rituals and festivities on this night were connected to mystical renewal rites of the Earth Womb and the birth rites of the Earth Mother. The turning of the wheel on New Year's Day was known as a time for purification, and the broom that Befana uses to sweep around the fireplaces of the homes she visits, while bearing gifts, is symbolic of clearing away the old, negative energies of the previous year and cleansing it for the coming new year. Other rites used for purification were burning effigy dolls of Befana to symbolize the death of the old year and the birth of the new year.

Italian anthropologists Claudia and Luigi Manciocco place the rituals of the Christmas Witch Befana back to Neolithic times, rooting them in the beliefs and practices of the ancient womb religion dedicated to the Great Mother of all creation. This feminine magic was rooted in renewal.

Goddess of Purification

Some sources suggest that the name Befana comes from Strenia, the Roman goddess of the New Year, purification, and well-being. This ties in with the tradition of *wassailing,* which is an Anglo-Saxon word meaning "be thou hale" or "be in good health." Intuitively, this is a sacred time for celebrations, blessing, and energetic purification.

Strenia presided over the sacred feminine rites of the New Year and would give gifts of figs, dates, and honey (foods associated with the blessed feminine essence). These feminine rites were full of joyful celebration and exuberance. In fact, Strenia's festivities were condemned by early Christians for being too noisy and licentious.

As part of the rites, on January 1, twigs were carried in a procession from Strenia's grove, located near her temple in Via Sacra, to the citadel in Rome. This goddess rite of renewal and rebirth is first mentioned happening on New Year's Day in 153 BCE.

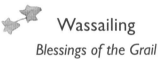

Wassailing
Blessings of the Grail

In Northern Europe, the traditions of wassailing—house visiting with the wassail bowl and orchard blessings—are intimately connected with forgotten Womb rites. Throughout many indigenous, shamanic traditions, the bowl is symbolic of the womb—a kind of holy grail. In wassailing tradition, this bowl of good health is carried round from house to house, containing a specially concocted elixir that each household is invited to taste and thus be blessed by good health for the coming year.

Linking this back to old tradition, this bowl is the Womb of the Goddess, and the celebrants are sipping from the regenerative cup of life itself in this ritual. It is also evocative of the ancient eucharists of the forbidden gnostic sects.

Wassail bowls, generally in the shape of goblets and chalices, have been preserved across the years. The Worshipful Company of Grocers, a guild in London dating from the fourteenth century, made a very elaborate one in the seventeenth century, decorated with silver. It was so large that it could be passed as a "loving cup" around the many members of the circle of celebrants in the guild. Some wassail bowls were more of a traditional bowl shape and carved from oak, considered a sacred tree.

 The Orchard Garden of Eden

Part of this tradition was visiting orchards, especially very old apple trees, reciting incantations and singing to the trees to promote a good harvest for the coming year and to wake the earth energies up. Throughout many traditions, the orchard is symbolic of the Womb and the sacred feminine, as are apples—such as the faerie realm of the Isle of Avalon, which means the Island of Apples.

Each ceremony varied from village to village, but the essence of honoring the feminine birthing principle for the coming year remained the same. Sometimes a wassail king and queen led a processional song that was played from one orchard to the next. The wassail queen was then lifted up into the boughs of the sacred apple tree, where she placed offerings soaked in wassail from the sacred cup as a gift to the tree spirits, while incantations were recited to thank the fruits of life.

In some villages libations of wassail were poured in between the forked branches of the sacred apple tree, symbolizing the magical yoni portal of the Tree of Life.

A folktale from Somerset tells of the spirit of the oldest apple tree in an orchard, in whom the fertility of the orchard is said to reside. In the tale a man offers his last mug of mulled cider to the trees in his orchard and is rewarded with secret treasure.

These seemingly simple tales contain in-depth alchemical grail lore within them. It shows that our ancestors did not take the bounty of Earth for granted and actively courted and celebrated the fertility of renewed life.

Women's Christmas
The Thirteenth Day

In Iceland, Epiphany is called the Thirteenth Day. Celebrations are held around bonfires with fireworks, as people sing tales of elves, giants, and other mythological creatures. Epiphany is celebrated in Scotland, Ireland, Lancashire, and the Isle of Man and is sometimes known as Old Christmas. In Ireland, Epiphany is often called Little Christmas or Women's Christmas (Nollaig na mBan in Irish Gaelic).

In Ireland there is still a tradition that for this day the Irish men take on all the household duties, while women hold parties or go out to celebrate with their female relatives and friends. In the past, women organized special high tea gatherings. Children prepare presents for their mothers and grandmothers. This alludes to feminine mystery teachings, where the wise women gathered together in sacred circles. In Latvia, young women make divinations about the future on this special day.

In England there is a feast called the Twelfth Night, marking the end of the Christmastide. People prepare a special Twelfth Cake for Epiphany, which is a womb-shaped fruitcake with a bean and sometimes other symbolical objects baked inside. The person who finds the bean becomes king or queen for the night. Traditionally, servants became masters for a night, and kings were humbled, and everything was turned upside down. This is reminiscent of goddess traditions and folklore where the goddess or queen disguises herself as a household servant or where trickster figures introduce chaos and bawdy delight to create wild fertility.

There is also a ritual of burning a piece of wood (known as the Yule log), which menstruates the old Mother Nature and invokes the doorway to a spring rebirth.

Epiphany of Feminine Wisdom

The word *epiphany* is often used to describe a visionary moment of seeing the light. Isn't it time we saw the light about the feminine wisdom ways?

Percolating all these various ancient traditions, it is clear as day that the period between December 21 and the New Year, especially January 6, was sacred to the feminine. Yet we have now forgotten the magic and mystery of natural life. Instead, we are corralled into consumerism, ushered into business, or we cannot see the roots of feminine magic and wisdom because of the heavy veils of patriarchal religions, which have sought to hide the Goddess.

We can revision a world where men and women gather together to celebrate and honor the incredible creative mystery of life, through which we were all birthed.

When we honor life, we can live in peace and harmony on Earth.

Wassail Grail Cup Ritual: Epiphany Blessing

To celebrate Epiphany on January 6 you can create this sacred rite:

☽ Find a bowl or cup to use in your ritual.

☽ Make a wassail elixir of your own invention (or look up a recipe). You can use herbal tea infusions and flower essences.

☽ Pray, give thanks, and make sacred intentions for the coming year.

☽ Make a special prayer for any situation that needs love.

☽ Either on your own or in a circle, sip from the Grail cup.

☽ Go in nature; sing prayers or incantations of your choice.

☽ Make an offering of the elixir of life to the earth or a sacred tree.

☽ Open your heart to renewed possibilities for the coming year.

☽ Invoke the feminine birthing power to bless your coming year.

FORTY-NINE

Nativity Mystery

Gateway of the Mother

The story of Solstice and Christmas are one and the same, with shared roots.

Nativity means "to be born": the Christmas nativity story holds a secret seed of the feminine traditions and is a grand mystery of what it means to be born or to be reborn. It holds the womb mysteries of how the feminine births life and how the cosmic feminine births new eras and epochs, from the cyclical Womb of time.

The nativity is archetypal and cosmic; it tells the story of how the sacred Great Mother rebirths the light of the sun-son and brings fertility and life from the feminine dark womb. In the Christmas tradition, this becomes our Mother Mary who births the avatar of the light, Jesus. It is an anthropomorphized version that carries incredible spiritual power. Whether we believe in a literal birth of Jesus or not, the medicine is immense. Once a year we celebrate the incredible miracle of a birthing woman and the magic of her child. This story is eternal; it lives through every human birthing mother. It also lives through Mother Earth and her birth cycles and the great cosmic cycles, as Great Mother births creation. This story is recorded in many sacred traditions around the world, where a cosmic creatrix is honored.

In old lore, the solstice is the start of the birth event—the crowning of the light—and it is on December 24 and 25, the eve of the Christ child, that the birth happens. After the light crowns through the cosmic cervix on the solstice, we enter three days of sacred birth space, a luminous passageway within the womb darkness, watching the light begin to emerge, as the birthing journey unfolds. When the light or child of light is born, a great celebration happens—with feasting, singing, carousing, toasting, gift giving, family gatherings, spiritual gatherings, and joy and hope.

Just like the family of a new baby might shower the parents with gifts, bring rich, nourishing food, toast with drinks, and take a time out of time to celebrate such an auspicious arrival, so this happens on a metaphysical level. Much focus is paid to fasting and retreat in religion, but in the old religion, celebrating was also holy.

Feasting, revelry, decorations, and rituals helped welcome the new energy, and if a new light or energy was not midwifed with joy and praise, it might not embody. The women's mysteries in particular were guardians of these sacred passageways.

Traditionally, the celebrations of the birth happen on Christmas Eve, December 24, or Christmas Day, the twenty-fifth. In the old ways, a new day begins with sunset, as it is thought the start of anything new begins first with darkness and the light only emerges later, out of this original primal womb. So at sunset on the twenty-fourth, the eve of the sacred day of Christmas begins, and it ends at sundown on December 25.

Then, thirteen holy days of celebration and revelry begin—the thirteen days of Christmas—until the birth energy is anchored on Epiphany, on January 6, when in the traditional story the magi and maga, astrologers and midwife-shamans, visit. This is probably related to magical practices of the witch midwives that are forgotten.

Yet these traditions did not disappear. They have been preserved, right under our noses, maybe not fully intact, but the magic is there waiting for us to remember.

A forty-day postpartum period is also marked out between the birth on December 24 and the returning of the light on Imbolc, February 2.

So we are not meant to race into productivity on January 1 or start new diet regimes or hit the gym. We are meant to keep close to the nest, nourishing ourselves, feeding this new light from the earth and cosmos, with yin magic.

How powerful that we still live the mystery of nativity, experienced by every woman who births and every human who lives within this great nativity of the cosmos and earth? And by intentional magic, we become a midwife of this light.

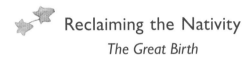

Reclaiming the Nativity
The Great Birth

After the birth of my daughter in 2019, this idea of nativity gained a new perspective for me. As a new mother during Christmas, this old, old story began to grow new green shoots for me, along with a deeper recognition of its significance, both at a spiritual level and on the level of remembrance of ancestral traditions.

Like many people who are not Christian, or have left behind any association with institutional religion, the solstice on the twenty-first had a fresher feel. It felt good to honor the cycles of the earth mysteries and welcome in a new cycle of light, while the Christmas holiday seemed mired in old associations and dogma.

Yet while holding a wee babe in my arms one night nearing Christmas, I found myself searching for secondhand nativity cribs online. I loved the cosmic idea of the earth rebirthing the light, but I also wanted the story of another human mother.

The image of Mother Mary, in a humble stable, breastfeeding her new babe, holding a miracle in her arms, born from her womb, spoke to my feminine soul. It felt intimate, personal, relatable. For many new mothers, the birth feels like a miracle: this new being, this new soul light emerges into the world, and everything around feels illuminated by this beautiful glow. I remember holding my baby for the first time, and the light shining through the windows felt like angels dancing.

We humans are story beings. We love a good old yarn, and we like it to be as close to our normal life as possible, not abstract. That is why so many indigenous and folk traditions veil great cosmic mysteries in everyday tales of normal people, and why quantum science and energies are portrayed as gods and goddesses, or beings just like us, who quarrel, make mistakes, fall in love, and birth babies.

There is a great cosmic mystery of how the earth rebirths the light through the womb of winter, and how even greater cosmic cycles ovulate and menstruate. It is powerful to recognize these vast powers and also to encode them in a story that we can make sense of and feel in our bodies, and relate to. As above, so below.

The nativity story holds these cosmic "mystery codes," and Mother Mary invites us into the stable with her, to join in the miracle of celebrating the birth of the light.

As the Dark Goddess holds the menstruation power, Mother Mary is the cosmic birther. She is the light twin to the dark feminine; they work in tandem, as a holy team.

Star of Bethlehem
Cosmic Mystery Codes

In 2020, we experienced the "Star of Bethlehem" again with a once-in-many-lifetimes conjunction, and it feels like we are being reminded of the deeper significance and mystery of the birth bed. Cosmic and human. We begin to see this not as a one-off day but as a journey, a pilgrimage.

That year, my baby's grandmother bought her a nativity scene hand-carved from olive wood in Israel as a gift, and we have it in the house illuminated with tiny lights. A friend of Sicilian and Polish heritage visited and was delighted by it.

She instructed me on some of the native folk traditions, woven around the Christian mysteries that were practiced for hundreds of years for the nativity. Rather than treat the nativity scene solely as a decoration, it is a *mystery play.*

I had set it all up beautifully, with Jesus in his crib and the shepherds and magi all gathered around, as the story tells. "Oh, no," my friend chided me. "Jesus isn't put into the crib until Christmas Eve on the twenty-fourth, *and* you have to swaddle Jesus, then put him away in a sacred place." The placing of Jesus into the crib is a family mystery ritual, performed on Christmas Eve with great reverence.

Likewise, the shepherds and sheep are placed near the nativity scene, as are the magi and their camels, as if they are pilgrimaging toward the stable. The nativity set *comes alive with magic.* It is not static; it is held in sacred time. It is a journey.

With deep magic, I have witnessed a real-life Star of Bethlehem in the sky on solstice *and* swaddled a symbolic baby, now nested in a small crystal shrine. I am waiting with anticipation for the night of Christmas Eve when he can be born.

As I sit here typing, I look over to the crib, and now in my mind, Mother Mary isn't just an inanimate carved statue but a *pregnant woman,* pregnant with possibility, waiting patiently for the great arrival. I can almost feel the "cosmic pregnancy" we have all been talking about, leading up to the grand conjunction.

And because I am a human being, an ordinary woman, I feel it more deeply through those magical little figurines and the story of an ordinary women charged with an extraordinary destiny—as are all mothers—to birth a new world into being.

Christmas
Celebrating the Cosmic Birth

So, in many ways, Christmas as such is not just an orthodox Christian event but a remnant of the great indigenous traditions that span the globe to honor the great birth mysteries. Solstice and Christmas aren't set apart as different traditions; they are joined together as one in the birth light.

They are part of the cosmic birth mysteries that have been forgotten, and dishonored, as a male story took hold.

The distinctly female aspects of the nativity have been overlooked or diminished, as have the feminine mystical arts of revelry, feasting, food, games, costumes, play, joy, community, domestic witchery, and sacred rituals of the hearth and home.

To illustrate this point, in England back in the seventeenth century, when Oliver Cromwell and the Puritans had taken power, a parliamentary law tried to ban the celebration of Christmas, considered as devilish. The law failed, but they did manage to mandate that the markets should stay open for business as usual on Christmas Day and not close to honor the birth portal and that church gatherings could not partake in any celebrations of Mother Mary birthing Jesus or enact special celebrations of the story. Even mince pies (a festive sweet treat) were banned as "popish indulgence"!

The same puritanical wave that simultaneously burned wise women at the stake was dead set against the celebration of this "popish" (read pagan) celebration of the feminine birth mysteries and tried to ban Christmas altogether, mirroring the numerous ways the feminine and her womb powers have been degraded as evil.

Over centuries this puritanism would also try to outlaw all traces of the pagan and mystical feminine traditions, including the festivities, gatherings, and holy days.

With this absence, the people lost their felt connection to the power of the cycles and seasons of life, unfolding within the land they lived upon, within their bodies and the cosmos, and enacted as simple and honorific family rituals in their home.

From top down, a religion of sin and punishment was imposed; but from bottom up, from the people, a continuation of folk traditions celebrating life was enacted.

For those of us with Christian cultural backgrounds, whether we are religious or not, the secrets of our more ancient folk traditions are hidden in plain sight. The magic portal of the solstice has been celebrated for millennia as a birthing mother.

In other traditions across the world, this feminine divinity who births the world is honored. The creation story of Aluna, as told by the Kogi tribe of Colombia and as discussed in *Womb Awakening,* is one of the most elegantly preserved transmissions that tells us of a *feminine cosmic creatrix.* Her menstruation does not indicate her sin but her fertility and her birth power. Her womb is holy ground.

> *The indigenous Kogi people of Colombia are one of the few living cultures that have maintained an unbroken connection to the deep feminine wisdom since ancient times, uninterrupted by the modern world. They are the spirit keepers of the most intact womb cosmology on the planet, and they have been told by Aluna, Great Mother, that now is the time to spread this knowledge to the world, as our Earth is at risk. They say: "In the beginning there was blackness, only the sea. No sun, no moon, no people. In the beginning there were no animals, no plants, only the sea. The sea was the Mother. She was not a person, she was nothing, nothing at all. She was when she was. She was memory and possibility. She was Aluna. She is the mind inside nature."*
>
> WOMB AWAKENING

We can imagine a time, long, long ago, when all cultures told this sacred story. Imagine how differently the world would look now if our birthers were honored? Imagine if we visioned Earth as a sacred birthing mother, too?

The solstice nativity was a sacred mystical time that our ancestors revered and celebrated with full heart and full participation. In 2020, we had our grand conjunction Christmas star; now it's time for the new birth. Let's celebrate the wondrous mystery of life and the Mother Earth who holds us and all the mothers whose bodies birth our new humanity.

May the holy birth spirit be with you, carrying the new light.

FIFTY

WITCHES' REBIRTH

Baba Yaga's Initiation

Hallow's Eve, or Samhain as it is also known, has always been a magical time of year. When I was a child, the possibility of witches flying the starlit sky was utterly wondrous to me. In my native, pagan north England, there was always the scent of the sacred in the air that night, as we donned our pointy black hats and, carrying our candle-lit, carved lanterns, traveled door to door, singing and playing music of magic and mystery.

The magic of this sacred eve never diminishes, and now this pivotal day in the calendar feels even more evocative, knowing as we do that it was once the Celtic New Year, representing the final turn of the seasonal wheel, descending us into the dark Womb of the Great Mother to prepare for the rebirth of light in the coming months. It is the time we winter ourselves to renew.

In Egypt, priestesses and wise women would also take to the cosmic skies on their broomsticks for forbidden shabbats of feminine ceremony and sacrament—as October 31 was the start of a three-day Festival of Isis, the Great Universal Mother.

In this spirit of wonder and awe at the cosmic feminine powers of creation and renewal, I want to complete our journey together by sharing a "Baba Yaga, Dark Night of the Womb" enchanted storytelling meditation.

Famously, Baba Yaga gave the gift of feminine magic to Vasilisa the Brave—the young maiden part of ourselves who receives power from initiation.

One of the magical tools Vasilisa has is a spirit doll gifted to her by her mother. This magic doll represents the soul of her maternal lineage, which she must feed and nourish as she grows up so that the lineage can assist her.

Baba Yaga tests Vasilisa so she can earn the fire of the cauldron; the primal anima, the shakti, the wild awen, the dragon power that transforms a girl into a woman. When Vasilisa completes her initiations successfully, the witch in the woods asks the young girl how she pulled it off, and she replies, "By my mother's blessing."

I believe this Russian fairy tale encodes an old knowledge of feminine magic, where a young girl experiences a sacred rite of passage to claim her womanhood, facilitated by a female elder.

Often these archetypes of crones, witches, and darkness represent the forbidden realms of feminine consciousness we are scared of. Yet these liminal root realms are where the wisdom, anima, and power live. By taking the path into the dark enchanted forest within, magic awaits us.

Baba Yaga is an archetype of the dark womb, and her roots go back into the Slavic Russian wild woods of mother worship—where she represented the wild crone, the feminine elder, the matriarch of the maternal lineage, and the wisdom initiations that come from journeying within the deep darkness.

Often we imagine Baba Yaga as a force outside ourselves, but she is also the voice of courage, wisdom, and fierce grace within us, who opens us to our initiations.

When we can trust her voice, we begin to own and inhabit the roots of our own power.

In this meditation, you will meet the wisdom crone Baba Yaga and the brave maiden *within you*. Both of these voices and powers reside within you, there to guide and initiate you. These archetypes teach you the wisdom to hold the flame, and that no matter what hardships you face, an invisible feminine spirit supports you. This spirit birthed the very essence of you with love.

So as you enter the dark woods, remember that this bright light shines within you.

You can sit quietly, light a candle, and read this meditation, pausing to allow the words to sink in and transport you into the wild woods, or you can narrate it onto your phone on a voice memo and play it back as an incantation, or you and your witch circle can read it out loud together.

Welcome to Baba Yaga and the Dark Night of the Womb

- ☽ Close your eyes, and allow the primordial silence to envelop you.
- ☽ Breathe into it, let go into it, melting into the vastness of Mother Night.
- ☽ You may feel Baba Yaga's wild presence flying through cosmic space, cackling and calling to you.
- ☽ Allow yourself to vision your body as a dark, magical forest. Visualize a doorway opening up in the crown of your head, where a sacred pathway begins.
- ☽ Feel the pulsing energy of your body, with your swaying branches and deep roots.
- ☽ Begin to descend and walk down into the dark pathway within. Walk slowly down through your head, your throat, down into the heart.
- ☽ Rest here and find your bright maiden self, Vasilisa—who carries the pelvic-skull of wisdom, empty with possibilities.
- ☽ Together, you descend deeper. You feel the magnetic, black pull of your womb, breathing you down. You keep descending, until you reach the edge of a clearing.
- ☽ You see a house on four legs, which spirals round a world spindle, holding the four corners of the world together as the house spins around with the moon. The back doorway goes into the dark moon, and the front doorway leads to the full moon.
- ☽ Inside this house is an oven filled with the fire of primal life force.
- ☽ Breathe into the gentle mist and the forest scent; feel your power pulse.

- ☽ You hear a wild cackle from high up in the starlit skies, and a wind picks up, spinning the gold and red autumn leaves into spirals of rich color.

- ☽ A wolf howls far away.

- ☽ You sense that your power is flying to meet you.

- ☽ Baba Yaga soars majestically overhead, her laughter full of promise and challenge.

- ☽ She is journeying in the stone curve of a womb mortar, paddling through the air with her pestle of power, riding the forces of creation with ecstatic abandon. Spotting you, the bright maiden, her eyes light up and her lips purse.

- ☽ There is a thread of light deep in your womb, linking back to the first ever mother, through an unbroken lineage of wombs. You breathe into this thread of light—drawing the strength, support, and love of the ancient mothers.

- ☽ Bearing your empty pelvic-skull, you follow Baba Yaga into her dark womb home deep inside. She gives you a message.

- ☽ Take a moment and breathe into your body to receive this message.

- ☽ And if you are ready, she lights the spark of fire in your pelvic-skull.

- ☽ Feel a fire pulsing inside your heart and womb.

- ☽ Pause.

- ☽ You are now ready to return back to the bright world. Your pelvic-skull is filled with the blessings of primal life force energy alive, fiery, igniting the wisdom thread of the Great Mother.

- ☽ Slowly, with thanks and prayer, you begin to ascend and walk back up the path.

- ☽ Feel this primal fire begin to spread through all of your body, warming you.

- ☽ Breathe gently into your body—right down to your toes and all the way into your fingers.

- ☽ Allow the sense of aliveness and warmth to sink into your bones.

- ☽ Place your hands on your womb and give thanks for your feminine power. Remember, the dark womb of Baba Yaga lives within you.

- ☽ You have been given the blessing of the Mother.

CLOSING PRAYER

Invocation of the Muses

Deep within the heart
Of all human beings
Sit nine muses, spinning,
Weaving their labyrinth,
Stitching worlds together,
With the red fabric of life.
Their wise old eyes look up
To see you standing here,
In the doorway of this book,
And with words of wild blessing,
They reach out to offer you
The red thread of their weaving,
For you to carry this memory,
And stitch it back into Love.

About the Author and the Illustrator

SEREN BERTRAND is an award-winning writer and the author of two classic books on the sacred feminine traditions, *Womb Awakening* and *Magdalene Mysteries*. *Spirit Weaver* is her third book exploring the worlds of feminine myth and magic. With a degree in English literature and modern philosophy, she weaves together mythology, spirit vision, symbology, and magic to bring forward the feminine philosophy traditions that once spanned the globe. She is informed by her ancestral lineage of old European witches and faerie folk and the later traditions of Magdalene and Mary who hid magic under their cloaks.

Seren grew up in the Old North of England surrounded by the great Celtic pagan traditions of well dressings and Beltane Maypole dances, where she was inspired by the Neolithic landscape of Mam Tor and the wildness of the moors. From a young age, she felt deeply called to become a visionary awenydd—a spirit keeper of the feminine stories. Her work is an expression of ancestress magic, our living legacy of love, passed down through an immortal red thread, from the sacred wombs of the ancient mothers.

www.serenbertrand.com • @serenbertrand

 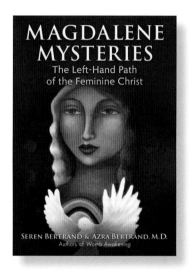

KATE MONKMAN is an artist who specializes in Celtic and faerie art. She is based in Scarborough on the northeast coast of Yorkshire, United Kingdom. In addition to her illustration work, she is also the author of the children's book *Maple and the Crystal Cavern,* a magical adventure story about mushrooms, nature, and the Wood Wide Web.

All the illustrations appearing in *Spirit Weaver* are available for purchase as fine art prints. The cover art is titled *Elen of the Ways: Path Weaver.* For more information about buying these prints and other beautiful craft works featuring the art, please visit:

www.freerangefaeries.co.uk • @freerangefaeries

Books of Related Interest

Womb Awakening
Initiatory Wisdom from the Creatrix of All Life
by Azra Bertrand, M.D., and Seren Bertrand

Magdalene Mysteries
The Left-Hand Path of the Feminine Christ
by Seren Bertrand and Azra Bertrand, M.D.

The Norse Shaman
Ancient Spiritual Practices of the Northern Tradition
by Evelyn C. Rysdyk

Shamanic Creativity
Free the Imagination with Rituals, Energy Work,
and Spirit Journeying
by Evelyn C. Rysdyk

Sacred Energies of the Sun and Moon
Shamanic Rites of Curanderismo
by Erika Buenaflor, M.A., J.D.

Healing Journeys with the Black Madonna
Chants, Music, and Sacred Practices of the Great Goddess
by Alessandra Belloni
Foreword by Matthew Fox

The Heart of the Great Mother
Spiritual Initiation, Creativity, and Rebirth
by Christine R. Page, M.D.

Speaking with Nature
Awakening to the Deep Wisdom of the Earth
by Sandra Ingerman and Llyn Roberts

INNER TRADITIONS • BEAR & COMPANY
P.O. Box 388 • Rochester, VT 05767
1-800-246-8648 • www.InnerTraditions.com

Or contact your local bookseller